COMPLETE COORDINATED SCIENCE

Chemistry

Stan Cooper   Will Deloughry
Mike Hiscock   Philip Naylor

HEINEMANN

Contents

What's chemistry all about?

Chemists have provided us with many important and useful products. The fertilisers and pesticides we use to grow our food, the medicines we use to heal ourselves, the clothes we wear, the cosmetics we apply, the fuel we use to run our cars and heat our homes are just some of these products. Many have been developed from the Earth's natural resources.

Understanding the properties of these resources and the physical and chemical reactions and processes that can take place is what this book is all about.

Obtaining natural resources . . .

The Earth is the source of many natural materials. The most abundant of these is water. Much of this water is in the oceans on the Earth's surface. Most of the other natural materials lie hidden below the Earth or below the sea. One of these is a thick, black, smelly liquid called **oil**. At first sight it might not seem much use to anyone.

. . . by mining or drilling

The natural materials on the Earth are not evenly distributed throughout its surface but concentrated in particular areas. Our ancestors used some of them, such as flint, for thousands of years. When they saw how useful they were, they searched for more. This was the beginning of mining. Some materials such as oil are not mined or dug up. The oil is trapped between rocks deep below the Earth's surface but it can be released by drilling.

Understanding the properties of these resources and the physical and chemical reactions and process that can take place is what this book is all about.

Making materials in the laboratory . . .

For a large period of our history the use of some natural materials was fairly limited. Until well into this century the major sources of many chemicals were coal and oils from plants and animals. Oil drilled from the Earth was largely used as a fuel for lamps. It is the role of the chemist to develop materials such as oil to their full potential. Chemists carry out experiments in their laboratories to learn more about how a material behaves – its properties. They begin to discover new properties which include chemical reactions to make new materials. These new materials have different properties and so the work of the chemist continues.

Oil is one of many natural materials found on our planet.

A drilling platform is built over the place where the oil lies.

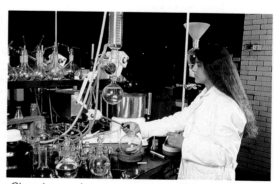

Chemists make many new materials.

2

. . . and on a large scale

Chemists may discover that some of the properties of the new materials they make in their laboratories are very useful. In turn, the chemical industry may want to make large quantities of these materials. It also wants to make them as quickly and cheaply as possible. To achieve these aims the chemist has to change the conditions used in the chemical reactions, such as temperature. When they are successful in their research, chemical plants are built. The new materials produced by the chemical plants are used by many other industries.

. . . to make a better world

Other industries use the materials produced by the chemical industry to make a better world. The pictures below show some materials the chemist has made from that thick black liquid called oil.

Chemist work in the chemical industry to make large quantities of new materials.

Cosmetics help you look better.

Compared to the properties of many materials, plastics are so much better.

1.1 All mixed up

Pure substances

All materials may be divided into two types: pure substances and mixtures. The simplest type of pure substances are called **elements**. Elements can combine chemically to form **compounds**. The elements hydrogen and oxygen, for example, combine to form water. These compounds are also pure substances but the elements are joined together in fixed amounts. Pure water always contains two parts hydrogen to one part oxygen. This is true whether the water comes from this country or from the North Pole.

Water is a compound. It always contains two parts hydrogen to one part oxygen.

Mixtures in the same state . . .

Mixtures are formed from two or more elements or compounds, which can be solids, liquids or gases. The alloy bronze is a mixture of two solids – the metals tin and copper. Air is a mixture of gases, mainly nitrogen and oxygen. Some drinks are largely a mixture of two liquids, water and alcohol. Look at the table of different types of alchoholic drinks. What does it show you about the amount of a particular substance in a mixture?

Drink	Approximate % of alcohol
Beer	3
Wine	10
Sherry	20
Brandy	40

. . . and in different states

Mixtures don't necessarily contain substances which are in the same physical state. Materials can be scattered as very small solid particles or as droplets of liquid or bubbles of gas in another substance in a different state e.g. a liquid. Special names are given to these types of mixtures. Many of the names you will be familiar with because such mixtures are often used in the home. If small bubbles of gas are scattered through a liquid, it is called a **foam**. If small droplets of liquid are scattered through a solid it is called a **gel**.

Coffee is a mixture of water and coffee grains or powder.

Aerosols are special mixtures containing small droplets of liquid scattered throughout a gas.

Emulsions

Oil and water are two liquids that don't mix. If you try to mix them, after a short time the oil and water separate as different layers. They are said to be **immiscible**. However, many foods contain mixtures of oil and water, for example salad dressing. Substances called **emulsifiers** can be added to the oil and water to make them mix. A stable mixture of oil and water is called an **emulsion**. Some emulsions contain tiny droplets of oil scattered throughout water. These are called *oil in water emulsions*. You will probably have come across these in household paints. What do you think a *water in oil emulsion* is?

One way of testing the type of emulsion is by adding **dyes**. Methylene-blue is a water-soluble blue dye. Sudan 3 is an oil-soluble red dye. A mixture of the two dyes was sprinkled on to separate dishes containing butter and milk. The results obtained are shown here. What type of emulsions are milk and butter?

Many foods such as mayonnaise are emulsions.

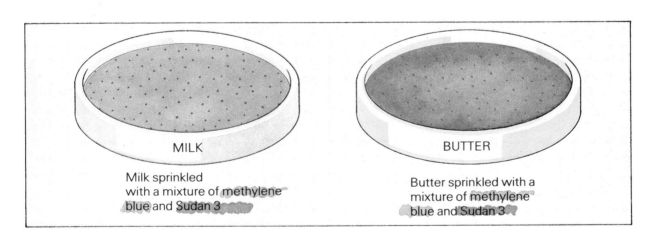

MILK

Milk sprinkled with a mixture of methylene blue and Sudan 3

BUTTER

Butter sprinkled with a mixture of methylene blue and Sudan 3

1 Which of the following are mixtures and which are compounds?
   a lemonade; **b** cheese; **c** carbon dioxide; **d** petrol; **e** milk.

2 Make a table of all the substances mentioned in the spread under the headings: solids, liquids, gases.
   Which can be described as 'pure' substances?

3 Give an example of:
   a a gel; **b** an aerosol; **c** a foam used in the home.

4 Why are aerosols not considered to be environmentally friendly?

5 Many perfumes are emulsions containing largely water, with the active ingredient in the oil. If a mixture of methylene blue and Sudan 3 were added to a perfume in a dish, draw a picture of what you would expect to observe.

6 Most cosmetics are emulsions. What type of emulsion (water in oil/oil in water) would be best for:
   a dry skin; **b** oily skin?
   Give reasons for your answer.

5

Properties of mixtures

We use different materials for different purposes. Bricks are used for buildings, wool is used to make clothing to keep you warm. Whether a material serves its purpose depends on its **properties**. A property gives you information about a substance. It might be a property you can measure such as how heavy or hard a substance is. This is called a **physical property**. On the other hand, it might give you information about new materials that can be made from the substance. This is called a **chemical property**. The table shows you some properties of two substances in a mixture. Do the properties of the individual substances in the mixture differ from the properties of the mixture?

	Sand	**Salt**	**A mixture of sand and salt**
Appearance	yellow powder	white powder	pale yellow powder
Addition of water	does not dissolve	dissolves	salt dissolves sand does not dissolve
Action of strong heat	does not melt	melts	sand does not melt, salt melts

Two solids, only one of which is soluble in water, can be separated by filtration.

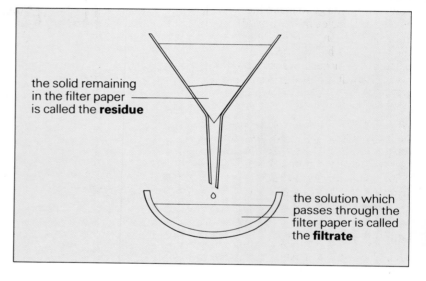

the solid remaining in the filter paper is called the **residue**

the solution which passes through the filter paper is called the **filtrate**

Physical separation . . . filtration

Mixtures can easily be separated when the physical and chemical properties of the substances within it are very different. Sand and salt is a mixture of two solids. However, they don't have the same physical properties. The sand can be easily separated from the salt by adding water to the mixture. This dissolves the salt. The mixture is then passed through a filter paper. The salt water is able to pass through the very small holes in the filter paper but the sand cannot. This technique is called **filtration**.

Physical separation . . . distillation

The salt water which is filtered off the sand is still a mixture of salt and water. However, the sand and salt can also be separated because they have different physical properties – the water can be boiled to remove it but the solid salt cannot. If the mixture is heated, the water will boil and eventually all of it will turn into steam. If the steam is collected and cooled it will turn back into undiluted water. This is called **condensation**. This method of separation is called **distillation**.

A desalination plant uses energy from the Sun to separate water from salt water.

Stopping things moving

When a gas is cooled, the movement of particles slows down. Eventually this causes the gas to stop moving around so much and stay in a fairly fixed position. When this happens the gas **condenses** into a liquid. Similarly, when a liquid is cooled sufficiently to *stop* its particles moving it freezes and becomes solid. By lowering the temperature to slow down the movement of molecules, gases become liquids and liquids become solids.

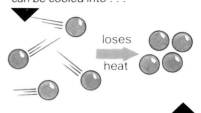

A gas moving randomly can be cooled into . . .

loses

heat

. . . . a more orderly liquid.

Making use of different boiling points

The difference in the boiling points of substances can be used to separate liquids from one another. The flask in the diagram contains a mixture of two liquids. It takes only a little energy to make the smaller molecules move around enough to become gases. When the mixture is heated the liquid made from smaller molecules boils first. The water cools the vapour and so vaporisation is followed by condensation back to a liquid which only contains the small molecules. So the two parts or fractions of the mixture have been separated because of their different boiling points. This process is called **fractional distillation**.

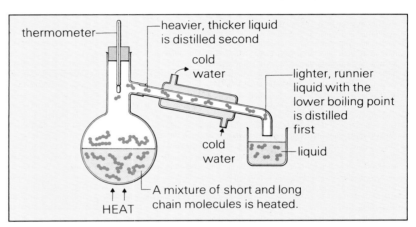

thermometer

heavier, thicker liquid is distilled second

cold water

lighter, runnier liquid with the lower boiling point is distilled first

cold water

liquid

A mixture of short and long chain molecules is heated.

HEAT

*Liquid hydrocarbon mixtures with different boiling points can be separated by **fractional distillation**.*

Looking at properties

The table opposite shows the properties of a group of chemicals called **hydrocarbons**. These molecules are made from hydrogen and carbon atoms joined together in a chain. The length of the molecule depends on the number of carbon atoms that make up the chain. The length of the molecule affects the runniness, **viscosity**, of a liquid eg. petrol is more viscous than paraffin. A liquid can be made less viscous by heating.

Even though these different hydrocarbons are each made up of molecules of hydrogen and carbon atoms their properties differ because the lengths of their molecules differ.

Name of hydrocarbon	Number of carbon atoms in chain	Boiling point °C	State at room temperature (21°C)
ethane	2	− 88	gas
butane	4	0	?
petrol	5 to 10	20 to 70	runny liquid
Paraffin	10 to 16	120 to 240	thick liquid
Lubricating oil	20 to 70	250 to 350	?

1 | Why does steam turn back to water when it hits a cold window?

2 | At room temperature in what state will the following substances be:
a butane **b** lubricating oil?

3 | Propane is a hydrocarbon containing 3 carbon atoms in its molecules. From the information given in the table above give an estimate of its boiling point.

4 | **a** What happens to the boiling point of hydrocarbons when the length of their molecules increases?
b Explain why the size of molecules affects the boiling point of a substance.

From the sea to your home

Crude oil naturally occurs beneath the sea or ground. It is an important source of many chemicals so it is much sought after. Once it is discovered it is extracted on a large scale by drilling.

Black, smelly and valuable

Crude oil is a sticky, black, smelly liquid that lies beneath the Earth's crust, particularly in areas such as the North Sea and the Gulf region of the Middle East. It is not very useful in its raw state but it is the source of many of the chemicals that we use everyday.

Nearly all the substances that are found in crude oil are **hydrocarbons**. These different hydrocarbons need to be separated out so that they can be used for different purposes. Look at the diagrams below and refer back to 1.2. How can the difference in boiling points of the various hydrocarbons be used to separate crude oil into its different parts (**fractions**)?

1000 litres of crude oil
- 2 l of liquid propane gas
- 300 l of petrol
- 70 l of naphtha
- 100 l of paraffin
- 300 l of diesel
- 20 l of lubricating oil
- 200 l of fuel oil
- 8 l of bitumen

*Crude oil is a mixture of compounds called **hydrocarbons**.*

Mixture	No. of carbon atoms	Boiling point (°C)
L.P.G. (Liquified petroleum gas)	1 – 4	−160 to 20
Petrol	5 – 8	20 to 70
Naphtha	8 – 11	70 to 120
Paraffin (kerosine)	11 – 15	150 to 250
Diesel	15 – 19	between 250 and 350
Lubricating oil	20 – 30	
Fuel oil	30 – 40	
Bitumen	more than 40	above 350

Crude oil is a mixture of hydrocarbons with different molecular chain lengths. As the chain length increases so does the boiling point.

Separating the mixture

At oil refineries crude oil is separated into its different parts by a process called fractional distillation. You may have used this process to separate liquids in the laboratory but as you can imagine the industrial process is on a much larger scale. The process is carried out in oil refineries in huge fractionating towers.

In a fractionating tower crude oil is heated by a furnace and the gases that are produced pass into the tower. The temperature is highest (about 350°C) at the bottom of the tower and lowest (about 70°C) at the top. The various gases rise up the tower, the smaller the molecule, the *lower* the temperature at which it boils. Those with smaller molecules, such as naphtha, will condense back to liquid near the top of the tower at about 70°C. Those with larger molecules, such as fuel oil, will condense back to liquids soon after the temperature goes below 350°C near the bottom of the tower. LPG will still be a gas at the top of the tower since it condenses at a temperature much lower than 70°C.

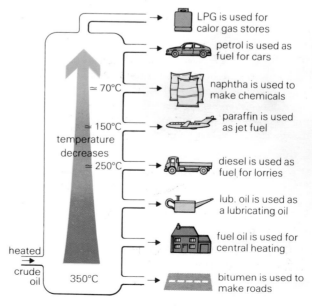

- LPG is used for calor gas stores
- petrol is used as fuel for cars
- naphtha is used to make chemicals
- paraffin is used as jet fuel
- diesel is used as fuel for lorries
- lub. oil is used as a lubricating oil
- fuel oil is used for central heating
- bitumen is used to make roads

≈ 70°C
≈ 150°C
temperature decreases
≈ 250°C
heated crude oil
350°C

Using the different fractions

In general, fractions made of larger molecules have higher boiling points and also tend to be heavier, less runny and harder to evaporate than fractions containing smaller molecules. What does the table show you about how the properties of each fraction link with its use?

The fractions have different properties. The different properties give rise to different uses. ▼

Fraction	Properties at room temperature	Use
Liquified petroleum gas	It is a colourless gas and is highly flammable.	Used as a fuel for calor gas stoves
Petrol	It is a free flowing liquid that is easily vapourised. It is highly flammable.	Used as a fuel in cars.
Lubricating oil	It is a very thick liquid that will only become a vapour at very high temperatures. It is not very flammable.	Used to lubricate machinery, moving parts etc.
Bitumen	It is a solid and will melt into a sticky liquid when heated. It is not very flammable. It does not mix with water.	Used to surface roads.

Small scale distillation

The apparatus shown in the diagram can be used to distill crude oil in the laboratory. A group of students carried out this investigation and found they were able to separate three different fractions from the crude oil. Their results are shown in this table. What do you think each of the three fractions contain?

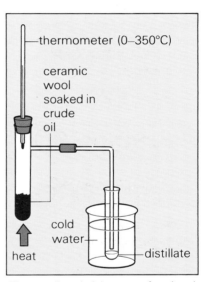

	1st fraction	2nd fraction	3rd fraction
Boiling point (°C)	20–140	150–250	250–300
Appearance of fraction	pale yellow runny liquid	dark yellow fairly thick liquid	brown and very thick liquid
How the fraction burns	burns easily with clear yellow flame	harder to burn with a smoky flame	hard to burn with a very smoky flame

The small scale laboratory fractional distillation of crude oil.

1   The table below shows the number of litres of some fractions of crude Arabian oil in 1000 litres.

      PETROL   200 litres
      DIESEL   300 litres
      FUEL OIL   450 litres

  a How do you expect the smell and runniness of Arabian oil to compare with the oil in the oil drum figure. Explain your answer.
  b What is the percentage of petrol in each barrel?

2   A fraction from the distillation of crude oil has a boiling point of 160°C. What properties would you expect it to have and what would it be used for?

3   **a** State one use of bitumen and explain why its properties make it an ideal material for this use.
  b Give two reasons why petrol is used as a fuel in cars rather than lubricating oil.

4   Look at the results of the simple laboratory distillation.
  a What hydrocarbon mixture is present in the first fraction? Give two observations that support your prediction.
  b Smoke contains unburnt carbon. Why does fraction 1 burn clearly and fraction 3 burn with a smokey flame?
  c Predict two properties of a fourth fraction.

1.4 Mixtures in solution

Useful solvents

When thirsty, you can choose from lots of soft drinks. Yet they are all similar, because they are mixtures of one (or more) substances dissolved in a particular liquid. Such mixtures are called **solutions.** The ingredients list of a soft drink will show you that the particular liquid is water; one of the dissolved substances is usually a simple sugar (such as glucose). Glucose is called a **solute** because it can dissolve in a liquid. Any solute needs a liquid to dissolve in before it can form a solution. A **solvent** is the name given to any liquid which can dissolve a solute. Water is a common solvent and forms **aqueous** solutions. There are other liquids (besides water) that can be used as solvents – these are called **non-aqueous** solvents. Because our body chemistry is based on having water as a solvent, non-aqueous solvents are usually poisonous.

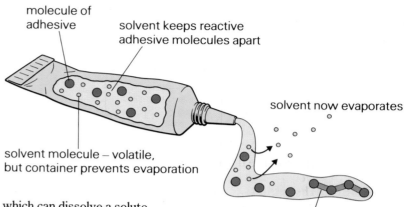

molecule of adhesive

solvent keeps reactive adhesive molecules apart

solvent now evaporates

solvent molecule – volatile, but container prevents evaporation

Solid adhesive left, which sticks to itself and other materials.

Arriving at a solution!

Glucose is added to drinks as a sweetener and also to give you energy. The glucose is present as millions of tiny glucose molecules. When all the glucose is dissolved, each part of the solution tastes equally sweet. This is because when solutions have been made, they produce **uniform** or **homogeneous** (evenly mixed) mixtures.

If you keep adding sugar to the water in a cup, eventually no more sugar will dissolve. Even crushing the sugar into tinier particles (or stirring the mixture even more) will not make any difference. At this point the solution is said to be saturated. A **saturated solution** is one in which *no more solute will dissolve* (at that temperature). The only way to be sure that a solution is truly saturated, is to make sure that there is always some undissolved solute present.

Solutions such as soft drinks are mixtures where all parts of the mixtures are evenly mixed.

Solubility

The food and drug industries produce many solid substances (such as sugar and aspirin) which contain **impurities** – these have to be removed before the food or drug can be sold. Often the food or drug is less soluble in water than a more soluble impurity. (An everyday example of differing solubilities is the way in which 'instant' coffee dissolves quickly in a cup, but the same mass of sugar dissolves more slowly.)

To remove a soluble impurity from a less soluble solid, just add a solvent (such as water). The impurity will quickly dissolve into the solvent, leaving the less soluble food or drug at the bottom of the container. The impurity will now be in solution and can be poured away; filtering and drying the food or drug leaves you with your desired solid – now without its impurities!

The amount of substance that can dissolve in a certain amount of solvent (at a given temperature) is called its **solubility**. The solubility of a solute in water is usually given as the *amount of solute in grams* that can be dissolved *in 100 grams of water* at a given temperature. A graph that gives information about the amount of solid that dissolves in a solvent at different temperatures is called a **solubility curve**.

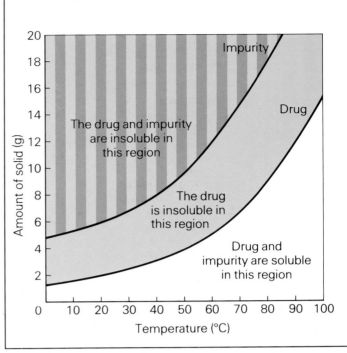

Solubility curves for a drug and its impurity. What happens to their solubilities as the temperature increases?

Crystallisation

To remove an insoluble impurity from a highly soluble solid, you need to use a technique called **crystallisation**. The solid and impurity are mixed with water and heated. *As the temperature increases*, more and more of the soluble solid dissolves in the hot solvent. An insoluble impurity will not dissolve, and is left at the bottom and filtered off. The solution of soluble solid (solute) and hot solvent is then cooled. As the temperature falls, so does the solubility. Less solute can now be held in solution by the solvent. When the solute can no longer be held in solution, solid **crystals** of the solute are formed.

■ Look at the diagram. How does the purity of the drug change after crystallisation?

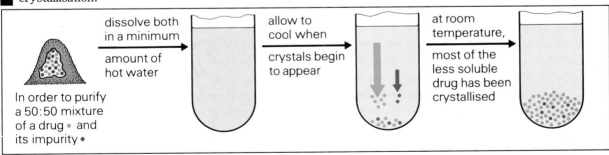

In order to purify a 50:50 mixture of a drug ● and its impurity ●

dissolve both in a minimum amount of hot water

allow to cool when crystals begin to appear

at room temperature, most of the less soluble drug has been crystallised

---

1 Why should non-aqueous solvents be kept out of the reach of children?

2 Give 2 other examples of mixtures which are solutions.

3 Why does each part of a *cup* of tea taste exactly the same but a *pot* of tea left to brew gets stronger?

4 Use the solubility curve to calculate the amount of the pure drug that can be dissolved in 500 cm³ of water at 60°C.

5 If 20 g of the pure drug in Q4 was dissolved in 100 cm³ of water at 90°C, how much would crystallise if the solution were cooled to:
a 50°C; **b** 10°C?
c Why do you never obtain all the 20 g of the drug by crystallisation?

1.5 *Physical properties of gases*

Investigating pressure and volume

A group of students used the apparatus shown to investigate how the pressure of a gas depends on its volume (when its temperature is constant). A footpump was used to increase the pressure of a column of air trapped above oil in the glass tubing. The pressure exerted on the air was measured from the gauge; the volume of the column of air was measured using the scale by the side of the glass tubing.

They recorded all their results in a table. Each student had their own idea about how pressure and volume were related. Which idea do you agree with?

Plot P against V since this is what we were measuring

When P goes up, V goes down so plot P against $1/v$

Plot both P and V against P since their product remains constant

Doubling and halving

From the results, you can see that if you *double* the pressure, the volume is *halved* – and vice versa. Gas pressure is caused by gas particles (molecules *or* atoms) bombarding the walls of the container.

How does the picture help to explain why the pressure is halved when the volume is doubled?

The bubble expands to $6\,cm^3$ (V_2) at a pressure of $100\,kPa$ (P_2)

At a pressure of $300\,kPa$ (P_1), the volume of the bubble is $2\,cm^3$ (V_1)

Boyle's Law *explains the change in volume as bubbles of gas rise to the surface of a liquid.*

Pressure (KPa)	100	125	200	250	400
Volume (cm^3)	50	40	25	20	12.5

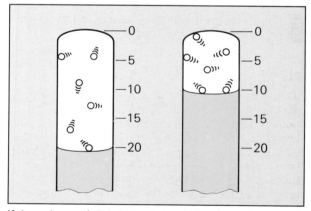

If the volume of air is halved, the molecules collide with all sides twice as often – so the pressure doubles.

The relationship between the pressure and volume of a gas can be summed up by **Boyle's Law:**

For a fixed amount of gas (at constant temperature), the product of pressure and volume is constant.

This is often expressed by the equation

$$P_1V_1 = P_2V_2$$

where P_1 and V_1 are the 'old' values of pressure and volume respectively;
and P_2 and V_2 are the 'new' values of pressure and volume.

Investigating pressure and temperature

If a gas is heated in a sealed container, it cannot expand – but its pressure increases. Pressurised containers such as aerosol cans are marked with warning signs about exposure to sunlight and temperatures above 50 °C because a build-up of pressure in the can could cause it to explode.

The students investigated the change in pressure due to temperature increases by using two identical round-bottomed flasks. Each flask contained air at a particular pressure. At the start of the investigation (at room temperature), one flask contained air at atmospheric pressure. The other flask had some air sucked out using a vacuum pump, leaving air at a lower pressure than Flask 1 (at room temperature).

The flasks were connected to a pressure gauge, then put in a water-bath. On heating, changes in temperature and pressure were noted. The graph of the results they obtained is shown above.

■ Can you suggest why the pressure of a gas is not zero when the temperature is 0 °C?

Pressure (kPa)	Flask ①	33	66	99
	Flask ②	20	40	60
Temperature (K)		100	200	300

For a fixed amount of gas (at constant volume), pressure divided by temperature (in Kelvin, K) is constant.

Absolute zero and the Kelvin scale

If the pressure of the gas at 0 °C is not zero it means the gas must still be moving and colliding with the sides of the container. In order to find the temperature at which the gas particles stop moving (so their pressure is zero), you have to draw back the line until it cuts the temperature axis. If you look at the lines on the graph above, you can see that this temperature is −273 °C. It is called **absolute zero**. It is often useful to measure temperatures from this point (to help with calculations). When temperatures are measured from absolute zero, the new temperature scale is called the **Kelvin scale**.

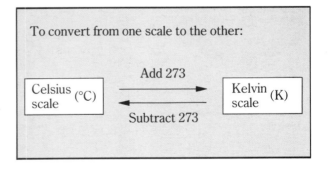

To convert from one scale to the other:

Celsius scale (°C) — Add 273 → Kelvin scale (K)
Kelvin scale (K) — Subtract 273 → Celsius scale (°C)

1 Sketch the graphs:
a P×V against V; **b** V against ⅟ₚ
at constant temperature.

2 Explain what happens to the pressure of a gas if the number of gas molecules is doubled, but the temperature and volume remain the same.

3 Look at the picture of the diver. What is the volume of the bubble when the pressure is 200 kPa?

4 Explain (in terms of the motion of molecules) why the pressure of a gas (at constant volume) increases with the temperature.

5 Look at the graph above. What is the pressure in both flasks at **a** 0 °C; **b** 100 °C?

At room temperature:

atmospheric pressure   ⅔ atmospheric pressure

↑ HEAT ↑

Pressure (kPa)

120 — Flask ①
110 —
100 —
90 —
80 — Flask ②
70 —
60 —
50 —
40 —
30 —
20 —
10 —

Temp (°C)   −300 −250   −150 −100 −50   0   +50 +100

| Temp. (K) | 0 | 73 | 173 | 273 | 373 |

1.6 *Heavyweights and lightweights*

Heavy stuff!

You can tell if an object is heavy because it is difficult to lift or carry. However, heaviness is a property of the *object* and not necessarily of the material of which it is made. You can compare the heaviness of two objects by putting them at each end of a see-saw.

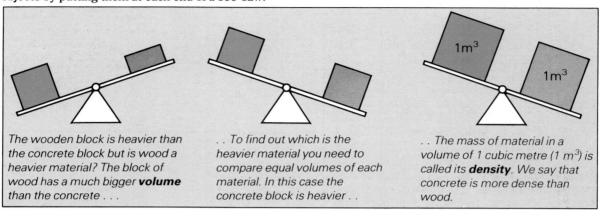

The wooden block is heavier than the concrete block but is wood a heavier material? The block of wood has a much bigger **volume** than the concrete . . .

. . To find out which is the heavier material you need to compare equal volumes of each material. In this case the concrete block is heavier . .

. . The mass of material in a volume of 1 cubic metre (1 m³) is called its **density**. We say that concrete is more dense than wood.

A dense situation

All materials are made up of tiny particles called atoms. The **density** of a material depends on the number of particles in one cubic metre and the mass of each particle. How does the picture help to explain why lead is the most dense material and sulphur the least?

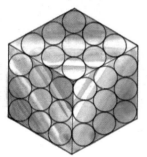

Metals such as lead contain heavy particles which are packed closely together.

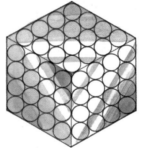

. . . Other metals like aluminium also contain tightly packed particles but they are not as heavy . . .

. . Some not-metallic solids for example sulphur, contain particles of about the same mass as aluminium. They are, however, not as tightly packed.

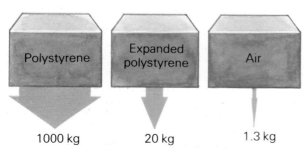

Polystyrene	Expanded polystyrene	Air
1000 kg	20 kg	1.3 kg

The density of materials can be altered by changing the number of particles.

Changing density

Materials can be made less dense by having fewer particles in a cubic metre or by replacing some of the particles by lighter ones. Polystyrene is a plastic material used widely in packaging as expanded polystyrene. Expanded polystyrene is made by blowing air into molten polystyrene. Look at the data which shows the masses of 1 cubic metre of three materials. What does it show you about the number of particles in *expanded* polystyrene compared with polystyrene?

14

Sinkers . .

Whether an object sinks or floats in a liquid depends on the density of the material of the object compared to the density of the liquid. Look at the pictures which shows you why an object sinks. What type of liquid would have to replace the water in order to stop the object sinking?

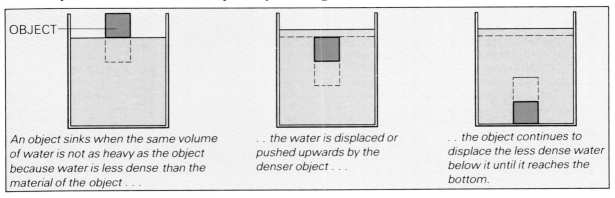

An object sinks when the same volume of water is not as heavy as the object because water is less dense than the material of the object . . .

. . the water is displaced or pushed upwards by the denser object . . .

. . the object continues to displace the less dense water below it until it reaches the bottom.

. . . risers and floaters

Rising is the reverse process to sinking. Look at the pictures which show you why an object rises then floats. Helium is less dense than air. What change would you notice if the bubble had been filled with helium instead of air?

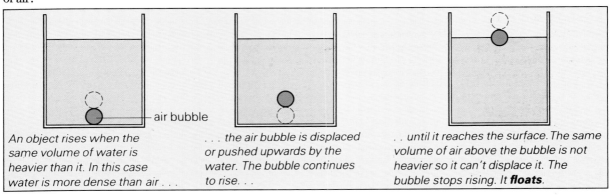

An object rises when the same volume of water is heavier than it. In this case water is more dense than air . . .

. . . the air bubble is displaced or pushed upwards by the water. The bubble continues to rise. . .

. . until it reaches the surface. The same volume of air above the bubble is not heavier so it can't displace it. The bubble stops rising. It **floats**.

1 The density of wood is four times less than that of concrete. What volume of wood is needed to balance a 0.5 m³ concrete block on the see-saw?

2 Why is copper a denser material than iron when the number of particles of each in 1 m³ is about the same?

3 Material A has particles 5 times heavier than material B. Material B has 10 times more particles. If the density of material A is 10 kg/ m³, what is the density of material B?

4 A block of lead, mass 100 g, was lowered into a measuring cylinder containing 50 cm³ of water. If the final level of water was 59 cm³, what is the density of lead in g/cm³? The same piece of lead was lowered into a measuring cylinder containing mercury. The level only rose 8 cm³. What has happened and what is the density of the mercury?

5 Look at the data on the densities of some gases given in kg/m³.

Helium	0.175
Neon	0.9
Air	1.29
Argon	1.8
Carbon dioxide	1.9

a If balloons were filled with each gas which ones would rise in air?

b A balloon sinks in neon but floats in argon. What gas could it contain?

c Breathed out air contains more carbon dioxide than breathed in air. When you blow up a balloon, why doesn't it float in the air?

d In a volume of 1 m³ there are the same number of gas particles. How many times heavier are argon atoms than neon atoms?

15

1.7 *Shaping up*

Do shapes last?

You have to apply a force in order to shape materials. This force can be such things as a pull or a stretch, a push or a squeeze. If you stretch a rubber balloon by blowing it up, it returns to its original shape when the air is let out. Materials which do this are **elastic**. Other materials such as plasticene take on new shapes. These materials are **plastic**.

Stretching . . .

A material can be investigated to see if it is plastic or elastic by pulling the material out of shape. Some students did this by hanging different weights on the end of a chosen material. They used two equal lengths of the material but of different thicknesses. They found that in both cases, when the weights shown were removed, the material returned to its original shape. *It remained elastic.*

1 **a** What do the results show you about the force needed when the cross-sectional area is 2 mm², to produce the same extension as a cross sectional area of 1mm²?
b In each example, divide the force by the extension. What do you notice about the results in each case?

. . . to the limit

The students then hung more weights from the material and obtained the results given in the table below. They found that with these heavier weights the force is no longer proportional to the extension and also that the material no longer returned to its original shape when the force was removed. The material is said to be plastic. Increasing the pull even more, makes the material go more out of shape until eventually it breaks.

When a material no longer returns to its original shape, it has been permanently stretched. This permanent stretching is called **plastic deformation**. The material under investigation, of cross-sectional area 1 mm², shows plastic deformation over the range 16 N to 20 N.

Area	Force (N)	16	20	24
1 mm²	Extension (mm)	85	110	—

Why do you think the students did not measure the extension after 20 N?

*Some materials are **plastic**. They take on new shapes.*

*Some materials are **elastic**. They return to their original shape.*

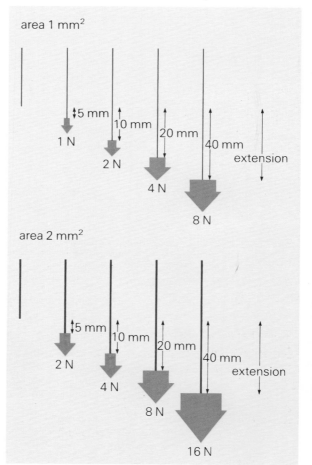

Can you see the relationship between force and extension? The force is directly proportional to the extension. As you double the force you double the extension.

Ductile and brittle

Materials which are capable of large plastic deformations are shaped more easily. Metals and some plastics can be easily shaped into useful objects for the home. Copper, for example is stretched out into long wires. Materials such as copper are said to be **ductile**. Materials which are only capable of small plastic deformations are said to be **brittle**. A brittle material usually breaks immediately when a small force is applied without first changing shape. Unlike ductile materials this means that brittle materials such as glass can be restored to their original shape by sticking the shattered bits back together again.

*Metals and some plastics are **ductile** when they are made so they can be easily shaped. Glass and pottery are also ductile when they are made but then become very **brittle** – they break easily.*

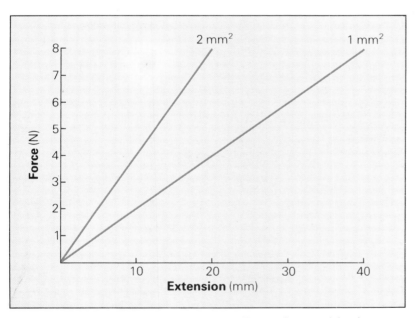

Resistance to stretching

Different elastic materials stretch by different amounts when a force is applied.

Stiffness is a measure of how difficult it is to change the shape of a material. The results of the stretching of the two lengths of material in the students' investigation were plotted onto this graph.

What does the graph show you about the stiffness of a material as it becomes thicker?

2 What is the difference between an elastic and plastic material?

3 State three things which affect the stretchiness of materials.

4 Use the results from the investigation to predict the extension for the same material when it has a cross sectional area of 2 mm^2 and heavier weights are added. Copy and complete this table.

Force (N)	16	20	24
Extension (mm)			

5 What would you expect the extension to be for a force of 8 N if the cross sectional area of the material was 4 mm^2

6 The **stress** in a material is equal to the force/cross sectional area. What is the stress in the material under investigation on the opposite page when the force is 4 N and the area is **a** 1 mm^2 **b** 2 mm^2?

7 The **strain** in a material is equal to extension/original length. What is the strain in the material under investigation of thickness 2 mm^2 when the force is 4 N if its original length was 1 metre?

1.8 Strength and hardness

Strong stuff

A strong material is one which is difficult to break when you apply a **force**. This force could be a pull such as a climber would use to test a climbing rope. Or it could be a squeeze like you give to an empty coke tin, or a crushing blow like a builder might use to break up stone slabs when making crazy paving.

A material which is difficult to break by pulling is said to have good **tensile strength.** One which is difficult to break by crushing is said to have good **compressive strength.** When materials are being bent, they are squashed and squeezed at the same time. To resist bending materials need good tensile *and* good compressive strength.

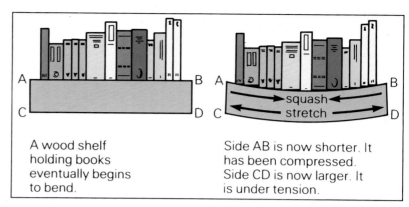

A wood shelf holding books eventually begins to bend.

Side AB is now shorter. It has been compressed. Side CD is now larger. It is under tension.

What does strength depend on?

A group of students decided to investigate how the length and thickness of wool alters its strength. The threads they used and the maximum forces they found they could bear before breaking are shown here.

> Why do you think the students were able to conclude that the length of the wool didn't matter?

Although the force varied for the threads, the force per unit area (e.g. 2 N/1 mm^2; 2 N/1 mm^2; 8 N/4 mm^2) or the **stress** was the same. The stress that a material can stand, provides a measure of its strength and not the force applied.

Look at the diagram showing the results of a compression test on a piece of concrete. What forces are needed to break the test pieces B and C?

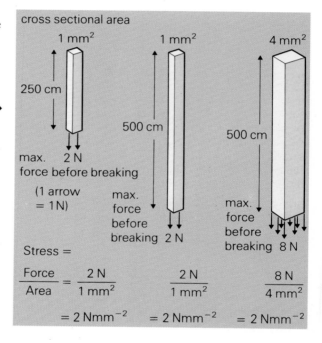

cross sectional area

Stress =

$$\frac{Force}{Area} = \frac{2\,N}{1\,mm^2} \qquad \frac{2\,N}{1\,mm^2} \qquad \frac{8\,N}{4\,mm^2}$$

$$= 2\,Nmm^{-2} \qquad = 2\,Nmm^{-2} \qquad = 2\,Nmm^{-2}$$

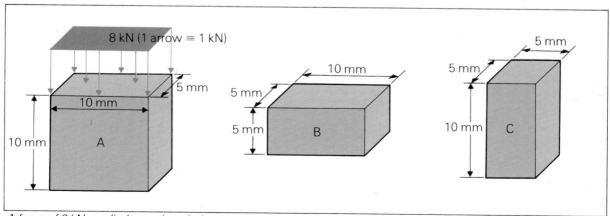

A force of 8 kN, applied over the whole area, was required to break test piece A.

What happens on stretching?

Solid materials are made of particles packed very closely together. These particles are held together by forces of attraction.

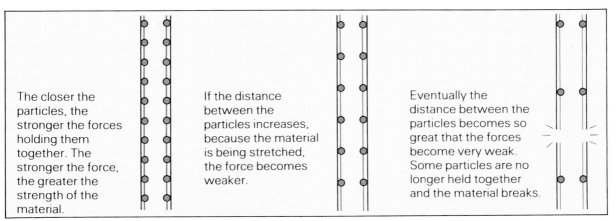

The closer the particles, the stronger the forces holding them together. The stronger the force, the greater the strength of the material.

If the distance between the particles increases, because the material is being stretched, the force becomes weaker.

Eventually the distance between the particles becomes so great that the forces become very weak. Some particles are no longer held together and the material breaks.

The forces of attraction between particles in a solid are weakened, eventually to breaking point, if the material is stretched.

Hardness

If the forces of attraction between the particles in a solid are very powerful, the material is said to be **hard**. A typical property of a hard material is that it is difficult to scratch. A harder material will always scratch a softer material so that the harder material can be made into a good cutting tool and will cut through the softer material.

Study the following information about the relative hardness of five materials then answer question 5.

Tungsten carbide will drill through **wood** and **steel**.

Diamond will drill through **tungsten carbide** and **steel**.

Wood can be scratched or marked by **glass**.

Both **steel** and **tungsten carbide** will scratch **glass**.

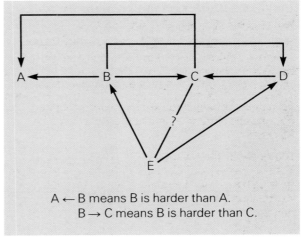

A ← B means B is harder than A.
B → C means B is harder than C.

The five materials, tungsten carbide, wood, steel, diamond and glass are represented in this diagram by labels A, B, C, D, E.

---

1 What is the difference between strength and hardness?

2 Look at the diagram showing the testing of the tensile strength of wool.
   a What force would be needed to break wool if its cross-sectional area was 2 mm^2?
   b Why would the length of wool change during the experiment? Would this effect the results?

3 A weight of 60 N has to be hung from a piece of polythene of cross-sectional area 4 mm^2 in order to break it. What is the tensile strength of the polythene?

4 a Why does a material stretch when it is under tension?
   b Why does increasing the thickness of a material increase its tensile strength?

5 a Is material C harder or softer than material E?
   b Identify the labels A, B, C, D, E belonging to the five materials.
   c Arrange the materials in order of increasing hardness, starting with the hardest first.

1.9 *Toughening up*

Energy storers and releasers

Many materials can store energy when their shape is stretched or squeezed but only elastic materials can release this energy and return to their original shape.

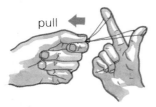

pull

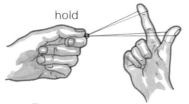

hold

release

If you pull a piece of string it will stretch a bit. But a rubber band will stretch a long way. Energy has been used to stretch the rubber band.

. . The energy is stored in the rubber band . .

. . . When you let go of the rubber band energy stored in the band can be used to propel an object. The rubber band returns to its original shape.

Tough and brittle materials-energy users

When a force is applied to some materials, they will absorb a lot of energy by deforming slightly without breaking. The energy is 'used' to cause the material to go out of shape. These materials are said to be **tough**. Other materials such as ceramic break easily when a force is applied to them. The energy is 'used' to make cracks grow bigger. These materials are said to be **brittle**.

The table shows a variety of tough and brittle materials. Are all the metals in the table tough materials?

Material	Tensile strength (MNm^{-2})	% Stretch before breaking
copper	215	60
concrete	5	0
cast iron	200	0
steel	700	20
ceramic	150	0
lead	20	60

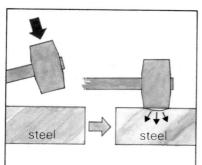

steel → steel

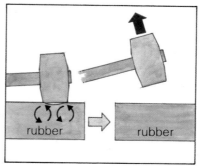

rubber → rubber

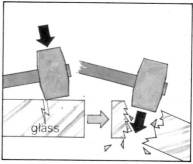

glass →

Steel is tough – it can absorb energy. The absorption of the energy causes the shape of the material to be permanently changed. Copper and brass are also tough materials that behave like steel.

Thick rubber is tough – it absorbs energy because it is elastic. The absorbed energy is released back to the hammer and the shape of the rubber is restored. Thick polythene sheeting and nylon are also tough materials that behave like rubber.

Glass is brittle – it is a poor absorber of energy. It can only resist a force provided there is no weakness in its structure. Energy from the hammer causes a crack, usually in the shortest direction through the material. If enough energy is supplied, it acts along the crack causing the glass to break. Ceramic tiles, cast iron and bricks are also brittle materials.

Toughening up

Brittle materials can be made tougher if you can stop them cracking. In order to do this brittle materials are combined with a material made of fibre. Energy usually acts on brittle materials by causing a crack across the shortest distance but with the addition of the fibre the energy is transferred through the material in a different direction – along the fibres. A natural example of this is wood which consists of cellulose fibres, which can be seen as grains in the wood, held together by **lignin** (*see 1.10*).

Using the same principle brittle materials such as plaster and some plastics can be made tougher by the synthetic addition of fibres. Its even possible to combine two brittle materials – as long as one is in the form of a fibre – and end up with a tough material! Glass reinforced plastic (GRP) contains glass fibre in a brittle plastic resin – this is an extremely useful synthetic composite, used for boats, storage tanks, pipes, low temperature engine parts because it is light and tough.

Wood is a tough material. It takes a lot of energy to chop through a tree trunk.

The bottom section of the bridge is being stretched by the weight of the cars passing over it. Concrete is brittle when it is stretched and can crack.

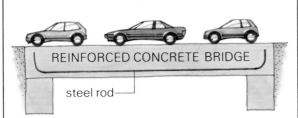

The steel rods act like fibres. Energy being used to try and crack the concrete is passed along the steel rods instead.

The principle of combining a brittle material with another material to prevent cracking is used in reinforced concrete.

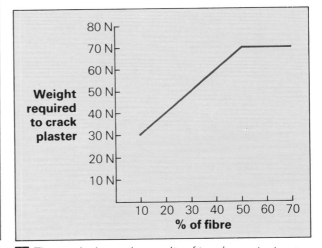

The graph shows the results of toughness tests on plaster. Why do you think the graph does not pass through the origin?

1. Give one useful example of an elastic material as an energy storer and releaser.

2. Why is it safer to have the front of cars made of tough materials?

3.
   a Which of the materials given in the table are tough and which are brittle?
   b Arrange the tough materials in order of toughness, starting with the toughest first.
   c Which of the following statements are true of the materials in the table? Tough materials are very strong. Brittle materials are very weak.

4. Do all tough materials go out of shape when they are subjected to a force?

5. Look at the graph of the toughness of plaster.
   a State three conditions needed to make the test fair.
   b What weight is needed to break the plaster when it contains a 20% fibre? b 10% fibre?
   c Sketch a graph showing what you think the result would look like if the thickness of the fibre was doubled in the plaster, given the same range of weights.

21

1.10 Rotten materials

You can eat apples but so can tiny organisms such as bacteria and fungi, causing the fruit to rot.

Wet rot is very easy to control when the source of dampness has been removed . . . .

Dry rot is harder to control because it can spread across brickwork and iron or lie 'dormant' for years.

Rotting away

You eat apples when they are fresh and ripe . . . but apples are also a source of food for other tiny organisms (micro-organisms). These organisms are so small you can't see them and so light they are easily carried by the wind from place to place – they are in fact all around us. You can, however, see a fungus when it multiplies rapidly from its spores on food. Fungi also feed on other materials such as wood and paper. When a material, such as an apple is being "eaten" by fungi and bacteria the material is said to be **rotting**.

Decayed wood eventually becomes part of the soil.

Wanted rot

Fungi and other micro-organisms, such as bacteria, are nature's scavengers. In damp conditions, they rot dead materials, for example wood leaves and manure. When these materials rot they are broken down into simpler substances which get added to the soil as **nutrients**. This is part of nature's recycling process. These materials, which can be broken down naturally, are said to be **biodegradable**. Many synthetic materials such as most plastics cannot be broken down by fungi or bacteria. They are said to be **non-biodegradable.**

Unwanted rot

Fungi will also rot the wood that is used in buildings. As a result the wood loses some of its important properties such as strength and toughness. When fungi land on a piece of wood they grow and throw out hollow tubes called hyphae. These hyphae are able to penetrate the wood. As they do they produce chemicals that are able to break down the materials in the wood into simpler substances. The fungi are able to digest these simple substances, allowing them to grow and spread further through the wood, and so destroy its strength and toughness further.

The two most common types of rot found in wood in buildings are wet rot and dry rot. How do you think they got their names?

Looking at wood

All plants need to stand upright to some extent so that their leaves can get plenty of light for photosynthesis (*see Biology book, 2.1*) Plants contain cellulose in the walls of their cells to make the stem strong and flexible. In certain plants a substance called **lignin** is added to the cellulose in the cell walls. These lignified cells are what we call wood.

Looking closely at the elements of the cells of wood we can see how it is such a tough and strong material.

The hollow cells of wood are joined together to make long tubes like drainpipes. This makes the stems of plants, like trees and shrubs, strong and rigid. ▼

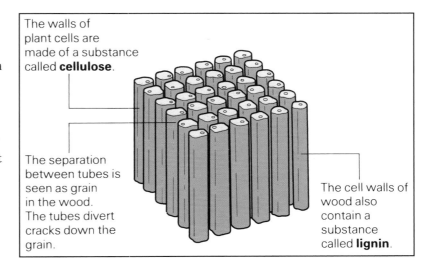

The walls of plant cells are made of a substance called **cellulose**.

The separation between tubes is seen as grain in the wood. The tubes divert cracks down the grain.

The cell walls of wood also contain a substance called **lignin**.

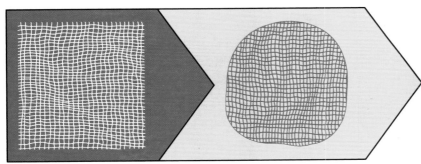

The cellulose forms white stringy fibres which are flexible and strong. When partly broken down they become crumbly.

***Lignin** is a dark brown resin. It cements the cellulose fibres together.*

Lignin makes wood tough and strong. The more cellulose fibres, the harder the wood is to crack.

Under attack

When a fungus attacks wood the hyphae of the fungus penetrate through the wood, boring their way from fibre to fibre so that the cell walls are partially or completely eaten away.

Fungus	Effect on wood
A	leaves the wood white and stringy
B	causes the wood to crack very easily
C	leaves the wood light brown but it cracks across the grain, not down it

1 Why is it very difficult to kill all fungi?

2 Why is timber left to dry out or 'season' before being used for building material.

3 Why is wood rot a problem and why is dry rot more serious than wet rot?

4 Why is plastic rubbish a problem and how might it be solved?

5 Look at the table above.
   a What is being eaten by fungus A? What properties do you expect the wood to have?
   b What colour would the wood be after attack by fungus B? Why does it crack very easily? What is being eaten by fungus B?
   c Why are the cracks in the wood attacked by fungus C able to spread across the grain and not get diverted down the grain? What is being eaten by fungus C?

2.1 The chemist's map

Decision time

You make decisions all the time. You make simple decisions such as what time to get up on a Saturday morning and important ones such as what to do when you leave school.

To help you make the right decisions about your career you'll probably try to get information from experts – the Careers Service, etc. You need to know whether the information is reliable before using it to make your choice.

Capricorn

(23 December–20 January)

Venus in Capricorn means you're going on a long journey. Some good news on the 15th means money isn't as tight as you expected. Forget spending wisely – buy something luxurious to cheer yourself up.

Would you buy a hifi and pack your suitcase on the basis of this information?

Finding patterns

If you're going somewhere new you may use a map to help you get to your destination. A road map shows an overall pattern between main roads and motorways. Once you understand this overall pattern you can use it to plan your route.

You may choose the quickest or the most scenic route or the one that avoids most of the traffic. As you get near your destination you can use a more detailed street map. You can see how the smaller streets fit into the larger pattern.

You'll find it easy to plan your route when you can follow an overall pattern in a map. ▼

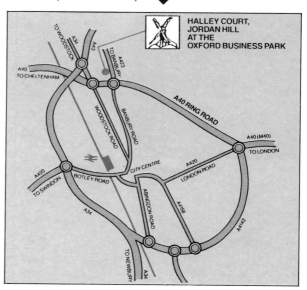

A chemical map

Scientists look for maps and patterns in the world so that they can make predictions.

Nearly 200 years ago, with the discovery of many chemical **elements**, chemists needed a map of the elements so that they could begin to find an overall pattern among them. However, it took chemists about 100 years before they found a pattern that was reliable enough to use.

Like the large road map you use to plan your travels, it contains more detailed patterns within it. And like using a road map, before you can begin to use the **Periodic Table** you need to understand what the patterns mean.

Potassium and copper are elements. As you will see later, they are both metals – but as you can see here, they react very differently with water. The Periodic Table helps you to make sense of the differing reactions of the elements. ▼

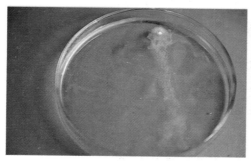

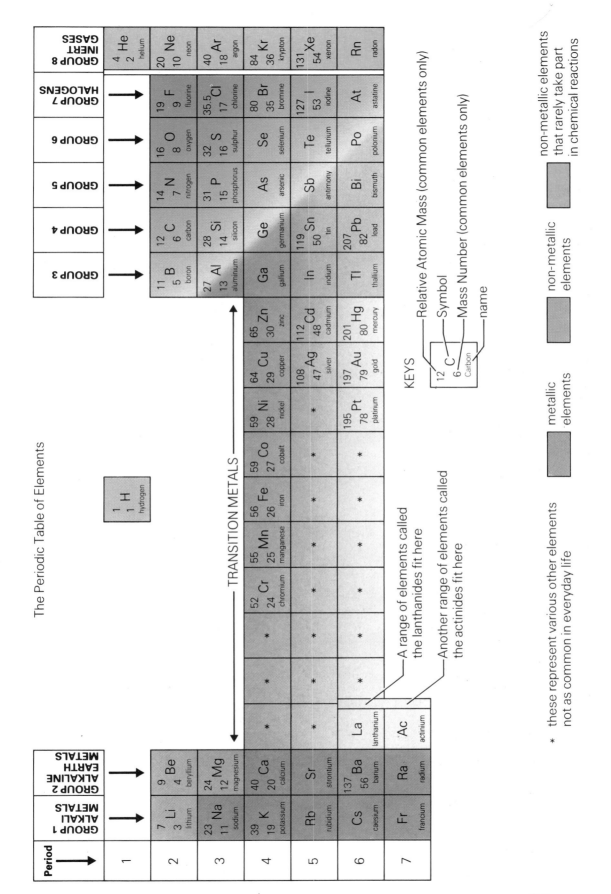

The Periodic Table of Elements

2.2   *Patterns between elements*

Elements and compounds

The world you live in is made of simple building blocks of substances called atoms. If a material contains only one type of atom it is called an **element**. Each element has its own special properties.

A few elements are found naturally on their own in the Earth or in the air. The element oxygen, for example, is a colourless gas which makes up about 20% of the air. Other elements occur in combination with each other, in the form of **compounds**. The properties of elements are different to those of their compounds.

Formation of oxides

There are 92 elements found naturally on Earth. All these different elements have different chemical properties. Many compounds can be formed by the different combinations of all these elements. Chemists look for patterns in the chemical properties of the elements so that they can make predictions about new compounds and about the properties of compounds.

Cement contains white solid calcium oxide

When fossil fuels are burnt in power stations . . .

. . . sulphur dioxide and carbon dioxide escape as colourless gases

To keep plants healthy, fertilisers are used which are categorised in terms of potassium and phosphorus oxide content

Animals take in oxygen from the air to react with foods. They breathe out carbon dioxide

Plants also take in carbon dioxide and water. They give off oxygen as a waste gas

When another element combines with oxygen it forms an **oxide**. Some oxides dissolve in water to form solutions which are either acidic, alkaline or neutral. The elements can be grouped together depending on the properties of their oxides.

You can measure the acidity or alkalinity of a solution by using a scale called the **pH scale**. **Acids** such as vinegar have a *pH less than 7*, while **alkalis** like ammonia have a *pH greater than 7*. Distilled water is not acidic or alkaline – it is **neutral**. Its pH is 7.

Elements which form soluble oxides can be divided into three types depending on the pH value of their oxide solution. One type dissolves in water to form alkaline or **basic** solutions. They are called *basic oxides*. Why are phosphorus oxide and sulphur dioxide called *acidic oxides*? What type of oxide do you think water is?

Oxygen combines with other elements to form compounds called **oxides**.

You can test the pH value of a solution by adding universal indicator. It will turn a particular colour depending on the pH value of the solution. ▼

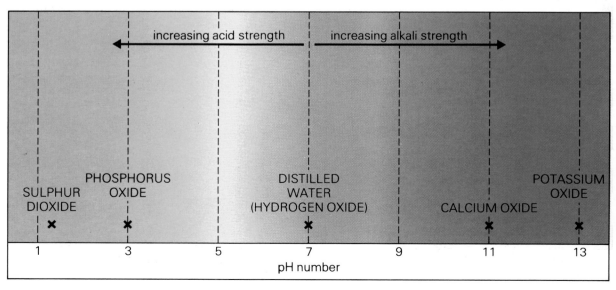

Metals and non-metals

You can see that the *chemical* properties of some of the elements, such as the properties of their oxides, are beginning to fall into a pattern.

Sulphur and phosphorus form acidic oxides whilst potassium and calcium form basic oxides. But do the same groups of elements have *physical* properties in common? Look at the data on some physical properties of the elements.

Elements which are good conductors of heat and electricity, and have a shiny appearance are called **metals**. Elements which are poor conductors of heat and electricity are called **non-metals**. You should now begin to see a pattern emerging. What type of elements do you think form basic oxides – metals or non-metals?

Element	Appear-ance	Good conductor of electricity	Good conductor of heat
Sulphur	yellow solid	No	No
Potassium	shiny metal	Yes	Yes
Phosphorus	orange solid	No	No
Calcium	shiny metal	Yes	Yes

The physical properties of metals are different to those of non-metals.

A special case

The element carbon is mostly found occurring in the Earth as a black, shiny solid called graphite. It is a good conductor of heat but a poor conductor of electricity. Why do its physical properties suggest it might be a metal?

If carbon is burnt in oxygen it forms a colourless gas called carbon dioxide which is slightly soluble in water. You can test the acidity or alkalinity of the solution with different indicators. Look at what happens to the colour of the solution when three different indicators are used to test it.

Use the charts, showing the colour of the indicators at different pH's, to decide whether this oxide of carbon is acidic or alkaline.

Universal indicator   *Litmus solution*   *Phenolphthalein*

Carbon dioxide solution turns different indicators different colours . . . . is it acidic or alkaline?

[Chart showing Litmus indicator and phenolphthalein indicator across pH number scale: 1, 3, 5, 7, 9, 11, 13]

Indicators change colour at different pH's. Different indicators have different colour changes.

1 Look at the first picture. Name all the oxides taken in by the plant.

2 Choose *two* examples to show that elements and compounds have different properties.

3 Give *one* example to show that in reactions elements in one compound can transfer to become part of another compound.

4 What colour would a solution, formed by dissolving sulphur dioxide in water, be if:
a litmus indicator was added?
b phenolphthalein indicator was added?

5 The oxide of an unknown element dissolves in water to form a solution which turns phenolphthalein indicator pink. Predict *three* physical properties of the element.

6 If a solution turns litmus blue and universal indicator green, what colour would it turn phenolphthalein? What would be the pH range of the solution?

7 State two ways that carbon dioxide can enter the atmosphere. Why is rainwater naturally acidic? Why does the burning of fossil fuels increase its acidity?

27

2.3 *Looking for patterns in elements*

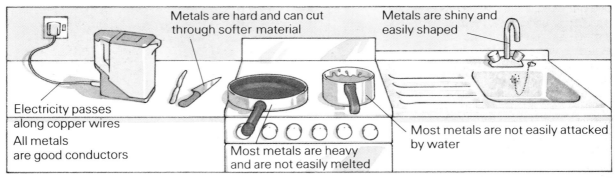

Electricity passes along copper wires

All metals are good conductors

Metals are hard and can cut through softer material

Most metals are heavy and are not easily melted

Metals are shiny and easily shaped

Most metals are not easily attacked by water

Most metals have several properties which are very similar.

Patterns in metallic elements

About 150 years ago chemists knew of the existence of about 60 elements. They tried to classify them by looking for patterns in their properties and the properties of their compounds. They knew that elements could be sub-divided into metals and non-metals (*see 2.2*). The picture shows you some typical properties of fairly common metals.

Some unusual metals

By investigating the properties of metallic elements chemists found some that did not always behave like other metals. One of these metals is sodium (Na). The pictures below show you how it differs from most other metals.

Two other metals, lithium (Li) and potassium (K), have very similar properties to those of sodium. So metals are not *all* alike and a small group of three metals has been found with properties different from other metals but similar to each other.

Sodium has a dull appearance because it reacts quickly with oxygen from the air but you can cut it easily to show a shiny inside.

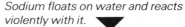
Sodium floats on water and reacts violently with it. ▼

Some non-metals can change the colour of universal indicator solution. Can you see any patterns? ▼

A group of non-metals

If there are groups of metals that have similar chemical properties, can other patterns be found in the non-metals? This picture shows you what happens to the colour of universal indicator solution when you add to it the four non-metals chlorine (Cl_2), carbon (C), bromine (Br_2) and sulphur (S). Which of these non-metals would you group together?

Making sense of the patterns

Are you beginning to see a pattern between the chemical properties of different metals and non-metals? The key to understanding this pattern lies in the structure of elements and compounds. In 1808, John Dalton, an English chemist, published his **atomic theory**. In this theory he proposed that elements are made up of tiny particles called **atoms** and that atoms of different elements can join together to form compounds.

Copper is made up of copper atoms . . .

1 copper atom joins to 1 sulphur atom to form copper sulphide

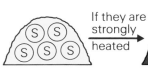

If they are strongly heated

. . . sulphur is made up of sulphur atoms.

Dalton and other chemists studied the *masses* of different elements needed to form compounds. The masses of copper and sulphur that react together are shown in the table. What does it show you about the ratios of the masses of copper and sulphur needed to make copper sulphide?

Mass of Cu (g)	8	32	64
Mass of S (g)	4	16	32

Since 1 atom of copper combines with 1 atom of sulphur to form copper sulphide, a copper atom must be twice as heavy as a sulphur atom. By looking at many reactions between elements, chemists were able to compare the **relative masses** of atoms of different elements. Then these masses were compared to the masses of a hydrogen atom, which was used as a standard. This gave the **relative atomic mass** (RAM) of the element.

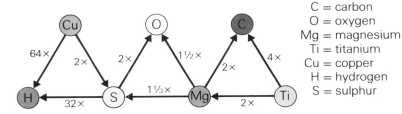

C = carbon
O = oxygen
Mg = magnesium
Ti = titanium
Cu = copper
H = hydrogen
S = sulphur

Cu →64×→ H Copper is 64 × *heavier than* hydrogen.

So the RAM of copper is 64.

Finding a pattern in the RAMs

In 1817 a German chemist called Dobereiner found a pattern in the RAMs of the elements. He noticed that when three elements with similar chemical properties were grouped together, the RAM of the middle element was almost or exactly the average of the other two. Although there were only a few such groups, his discovery provided a link between the RAM of an element and its properties.

Element	Relative atomic mass (RAM)
Li	7
Na	23
K	39

What do you notice about the RAM of Na compared to those of Li and K?

1 State *three* ways in which potassium behaves as **a** a typical metal **b** an unusual metal

2 What evidence do you have that chlorine can be used as a household bleach?

3 The table below shows some masses of iron and sulphur that react to form iron sulphide. Assuming 1 atom of iron reacts with 1 atom of sulphur
   a Fill in the gaps
   b What is the RAM of iron?

Mass of Fe (g)	14	?	560
Mass of S (g)	?	64	320

4 Use the information in the figure above to find out the RAM of oxygen, titanium, magnesium and carbon.

5 The elements S, Se and Te follow Dobereiner's pattern for RAMs. The RAM of S is 32 and the RAM of Te is 128. What is the approximate RAM of Se?

6 Below is a list of elements and their respective RAMs. Which three do you predict would have the same properties?

Element	Si	Ca	Cu	Sr	Ba
RAM	28	40	64	88	137

2.4 Understanding the patterns

Mendeleev's periodic table

At the beginning of the nineteenth century, chemists had already established patterns between certain elements. You can read more about this on 2.2 and 2.3. The search for new patterns continued for the next fifty years. In 1869 a Russian chemist, called Mendeleev, arranged all the elements which were known in order of increasing relative atomic masses. The table below shows you how he did this. He arranged the elements in horizontal **periods** and eight columns called **groups**. Mendeleev found that elements in the *same group* had similar chemical properties. This repetition of properties is called *periodic* and so the table became known as the **Periodic Table**.

Dimitri Ivanovitch Mendeleev (1834–1907) was the founder of the modern Periodic Table.

Part of Mendeleev's Periodic Table. Elements with similar properties occur at regular intervals in the table when arranged in order of increasing RAMs.

← GROUP →

PERIOD ↓	1	2	3	4	5	6	7	8
1	^{1}H							
2	^{7}Li	^{13}Be	^{11}B	^{12}C	^{14}N	^{16}O	^{19}F	
3	^{23}Na	^{24}Mg	^{27}Al	^{28}Si	^{31}P	^{32}S	^{35}Cl	
4	^{39}K	^{40}Ca						^{56}Fe ^{39}Ni ^{59}Co
5				*			^{80}Bi	
6								
7				^{118}Sn		^{128}Te	^{127}I	
8								
9								
10								
11				^{207}Pb				
12								

The proof of the pudding . . .

Mendeleev's table contained a separate group – Group 8 – for elements that did not fit into his arrangement. He also left gaps – indicated by * – if no known element fitted the space. He realised that if the table was to be of value, he should be able to predict some of the properties of these missing elements. Look at the graph which shows you how the density of two metallic elements in Group 4 changes with their RAM. If you assume that the missing element in Group 4 together with Sn (tin) and Pb (lead) form one of Dobereiner's three-element groups (*see 2.3*) what would you predict the RAM and density of the missing element to be?

Mendeleev called this missing Group 4 element ekasilicon but it is now called germanium. When it was eventually discovered it was found to have a RAM of 73 and density of 5.3 g/cm³. Does it fit the graphical relationship?

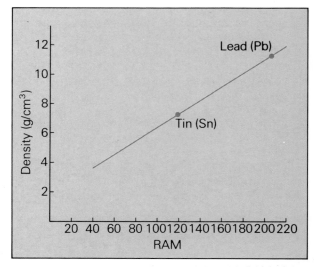

The graph shows the change in density with RAM of the metallic elements Sn and Pb in Group 4.

... is in the atomic numbers

Although Mendeleev's table proved very useful in predicting properties, there were problems. Elements with RAMs that did not fit were being forced into wrong positions. Look at Groups 6 and 7 in Mendeleev's table. He placed iodine after tellurium because its properties were similar to the other elements in that group. Also no place could be found for the noble gases argon, helium, neon, krypton and xenon, when they were discovered in the 1890s. Mendeleev and other scientists needed new knowledge to sort out these problems. The puzzle was solved by the discovery of the sub-atomic particle – the **electron** – at the beginning of this century.

The atom was found to consist of a central core or **nucleus** surrounded by particles called electrons. Atoms of different elements contain different numbers of electrons. The number of electrons in the atom of an element is the same as its **atomic number**. By rearranging the Periodic Table in order of *increasing atomic number* instead of RAMs, the problems of elements in wrong positions and where to put the noble gases were solved.

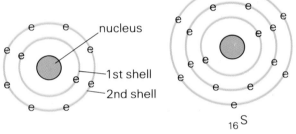

PERIOD ↓	6	7	8
1			$_2$He
2	$_8$O	$_9$F	$_{10}$Ne
3	$_{16}$S	$_{19}$Cl	
4		$_{35}$Br	
5			
6			
7	$_{52}$Te	$_{53}$I	

←GROUP→

Iodine comes after tellurium when Mendeleev's table is rearranged in order of atomic number instead of RAMs. Where have the noble gases been found to fit?

The key – outer shell electrons

Although the arrangement of elements in order of increasing atomic number put elements in their correct places, it did not explain why they should be in particular groups. But this *is* explained by the arrangement of the electrons in energy levels or **shells** around the nucleus of an atom. Each shell can only hold a definite number of electrons [1st shell: 2, 2nd shell: 8, 3rd shell: 8 . . .] but the outer shell isn't always full. Elements in the same group have the same *number of electrons* in their outer shell.

nucleus
1st shell
2nd shell

$_{10}$Ne

$_{16}$S

The noble gases were found to be very unreactive. Neon, with an atomic number of 10, has 10 electrons surrounding the nucleus. The first shell contains 2 electrons and the second shell 8 electrons. Both shells are full. An electronic structure with only full shells is said to be stable.

Most atoms are like sulphur with only partly filled outer shells. Sulphur has 16 electrons and an electronic structure 2,8,6. This means it has 2 electrons in the first shell (full), 8 in its second shell (full) and 6 in its third (not full). Oxygen has an electronic structure 2,6. It is in the same group as sulphur.

1. Look at Mendeleev's table. Which other element besides iodine is out of place?

2. Below are some properties of three elements in Group 4. Use this information to predict the corresponding properties of germanium.

Element	Appearance	Appearance of oxide
Carbon	dark grey	colourless gas
Silicon	dark grey	white powder
Tin	light grey	white powder

3. What do you think happened to the elements Fe, Co and Ni in Group 8 of Mendeleev's table?

4. The noble gas after He and Ne is argon (Ar). What do you think its atomic number and electronic structure are?

5. Use the figure above to work out the electronic structures of fluorine (F) and chlorine (Cl). What is the relationship between the number of outer shell electrons and the group to which an element belongs?

6. In what ways is the modern Periodic Table *different to* and *the same as* Mendeleev's? Look back to 2.1.

YOU CAN READ MORE ABOUT ATOMIC NUMBER AND STRUCTURE ON SPREAD 3.2.

GROUP 1

$_3$ Li
$_{11}$ Na
$_{19}$ K
$_{37}$ Rb
$_{55}$ Cs
$_{87}$ Fr

Physical patterns

Like all metals, the elements in Group 1 are good conductors of heat and electricity. However, they are not typical metals (*see 2.3*). Look at the table opposite. Which metal in the group would you predict to have the lowest melting point?

Element	RAM	Melting Point (°C)	Size of atom (nm)
Li	7	180	0.133
K	39	64	0.203
Na	23	98	0.157

Some physical properties of the three most common elements in Group 1.

Chemical patterns – reactions with oxygen and chlorine . . .

Group 1 contains the most reactive metals in the Periodic Table. These alkali metals are dull in appearance because their shiny surfaces react quickly with oxygen from the air. When one of these metals reacts with oxygen a metal oxide is formed which has the general formula M_2O – M stands for any alkali metal. For example, sodium (Na) combines with oxygen to form sodium oxide, Na_2O.

Sodium + oxygen → sodium oxide
$$4Na + O_2 \rightarrow 2Na_2O$$

Chlorine reacts with the Group 1 metals to form metal chlorides with the general formula MCl. For example, potassium combines with chlorine to form potassium chloride, KCl.

Potassium + chlorine → potassium chloride
$$2K + Cl_2 \rightarrow 2KCl$$

The pictures show you the reaction of some Group 1 metals with chlorine. What do they show you about the reactivity of the metals as you go down Group 1?

There is a fairly energetic reaction between lithium and chlorine to form a white solid Li Cl.

Sodium reacts energetically with Cl_2 to produce white NaCl.

. . . with water

Lithium, sodium and potassium all react similarly with cold water. They skim across its surface and react vigorously, producing hydrogen gas. The metals eventually dissolve to produce an alkaline solution – this is why they are often referred to as the alkali metals – containing the metal hydroxide, MOH.

Sodium reacts with water releasing hydrogen gas and producing an alkaline solution containing sodium hydroxide, NaOH.

Sodium + water → sodium hydroxide + hydrogen
$$2Na + 2H_2O \rightarrow 2NaOH + H_2$$

The reaction of different alkali metals with water is very similar but the reactivity depends on the particular metal. These three pictures show lithium, sodium and potassium reacting with cold water. Which is which? ▼

Explaining the patterns

Size
Each atom has a nucleus containing positive particles called **protons**. Surrounding the nucleus are negatively charged particles called **electrons** (*see 2.4*). In any atom there are *the same number* of protons and electrons. Its overall charge is balanced ▶ The electrons are arranged around the nucleus in energy levels or shells (*see 2.4*). Look at the diagrams of the lithium and sodium atoms. Can you explain why the size of the atoms increases as you go down the group?

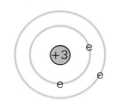

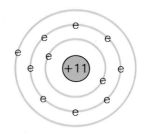

The Li atom has 3 protons in the nucleus and 3 electrons which are in two shells. It has the electronic structure 2,1.

The Na atom has 11 protons in the nucleus and 11 electrons which are in three shells. It has the electronic structure 2,8,1.

Reactions
When atoms of some elements are involved in chemical reactions, they obtain **stable** electronic structures like those of the noble gases (*see 2.4*) – all their electron shells are full. Since alkali metals all have one electron in their outer shell, they obtain full shells in the same way as each other – so they have similar chemical reactions.

Reactivity
The reactivity of an alkali metal is a measure of how easily it loses its 1 outer shell electron. The more easily the electron is lost, the more reactive the alkali metal is. The positively charged protons in the nucleus of the atom attract the negatively charged electrons in the shells, keeping them in their shells. However, the further away the electrons are from the nucleus, the less strongly they are held in attraction to the positive nucleus. Also, the outer shell electrons are shielded from the positive charge in the nucleus by the inner shells of electrons. How do the diagrams ▶ explain why sodium is more reactive than lithium?

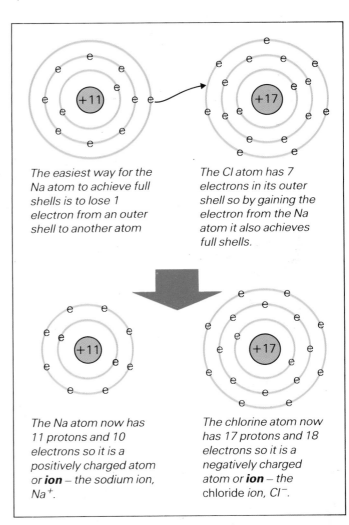

The easiest way for the Na atom to achieve full shells is to lose 1 electron from an outer shell to another atom

The Cl atom has 7 electrons in its outer shell so by gaining the electron from the Na atom it also achieves full shells.

The Na atom now has 11 protons and 10 electrons so it is a positively charged atom or **ion** – the sodium ion, Na$^+$.

The chlorine atom now has 17 protons and 18 electrons so it is a negatively charged atom or **ion** – the chloride ion, Cl$^-$.

1. The force of attraction between metal atoms decreases as their size increases. Explain why the melting point of the metals decreases as you go down the group.

2. Write a symbol equation for the reaction between rubidium and water. Describe what you would expect to observe if you added rubidium to cold water.

3. Write down the symbol and electronic structure of the ion formed when lithium loses 1 electron.

4. What precautions do you think you should take when using an alkali metal?

5. Draw a diagram of the potassium atom. Explain why it is more reactive than sodium but less reactive than caesium.

6. Write down as many similarities as you can find between the chemistry of the elements sodium and potassium and their compounds.

7. Find the metals Be, Mg and Ca in the Periodic Table.
   a What group are they in and how many electrons do they have in their outer shells?
   b Predict what happens to the size of the atoms and their reactivity as you go down the group.

GROUP 7

$_9F$
$_{17}Cl$
$_{35}Br$
$_{53}I$

Physical patterns

Most metals are very similar in appearance – not so with non-metals. One of the most striking features of the non-metal halogens in Group 7 is that at room temperature they don't appear to have much in common.

Look at the picture of the three most common halogens – chlorine, bromine and iodine. Would you expect fluorine to be a gas, solid or liquid at room temperature?

At room temperature chlorine is a greenish yellow gas, bromine a reddish brown liquid and iodine a shiny black solid.

Bleaching action

You may know that chlorine and its compounds are used as household bleaches to remove stains and colour from dyes. Other halogens can also be used as bleaches. The pictures show you what happens when you add three halogens to water containing universal indicator. What does this show you about the reactivity of the halogens as you go down the group?

You can see that the addition of chlorine to the indicator has quickly bleached the indicator. Sometimes you may even see the indicator turn red first, showing that an acidic solution has been formed (*see 2.2*). Chlorine reacts with water to form a solution containing two acids: hydrochloric acid (HCl) and hypochlorous acid (HCIO). The red colour of the indicator is quickly lost because HCIO is such a good bleaching agent!

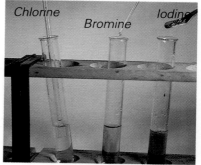

Colour of indicator after 2 minutes.

Chlorine + water → hydrochloric acid + hypochlorous acid
$$Cl_2 + H_2O \rightarrow HCl + HClO$$

Bromine (Br_2) and iodine (I_2) react with water in a similar way but much more slowly. Fluorine is the most reactive element known but reacts with the water in a different way and does not produce a bleach.

Household bleaches

Most household bleaches are made by the reaction between chlorine and sodium hydroxide. This produces a solution containing sodium hypochlorite (NaClO) which is a good bleaching agent.

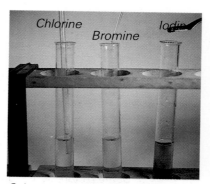

Colour of indicator after 10+ minutes.

Chlorine + sodium hydroxide → sodium chloride
                                + sodium hypochlorite + water

$$Cl_2 + 2NaOH \rightarrow NaCl + NaClO + H_2O$$

Halogens are also used as chemical agents to kill germs. This also shows their different reactivities. Chlorine is used as a germicide in swimming baths but it is too reactive to use as a germicide on open skin wounds. People used a mild antiseptic containing iodine dissolved in alcohol – *tincture of iodine* – for this because it is less reactive.

This label shows some of the safety factors you should take note of when you use bleaches for cleaning. What else is this type of bleach used for?

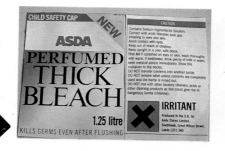

Displacement reactions

You can confirm the order of reactivity of the halogens by looking at their **displacement reactions**. A displacement reaction is one in which the more reactive element 'pushes out' or *displaces* the less reactive element. This means a more reactive halogen such as chlorine should displace a less reactive halogen such as iodine from one of its compounds. You can check the halogen present at the end of the reaction by using a suitable solvent.

The pictures below show you what happens when chlorine is added to potassium bromide solution and to potassium iodide solution.

When chlorine is bubbled into potassium bromide solution, the less reactive bromine is displaced by the more reactive chlorine.

Potassium bromide + chlorine → potassium chloride + bromine
$$2KBr + Cl_2 \rightarrow 2KCl + Br_2$$

However, if iodine is added to potassium bromide solution, the less reactive iodine is *not* able to displace the more reactive bromine.

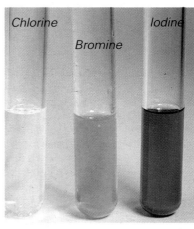

Chlorine   Iodine
Bromine

Halogens will dissolve in suitable solvents such as trichloromethane to give characteristic colours.

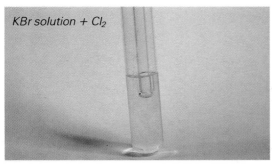

KBr solution + Cl₂

Add
→
trichloro-
methane
solvent

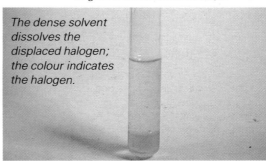

The dense solvent dissolves the displaced halogen; the colour indicates the halogen.

KI solution + Cl₂

Add
→
trichloro-
methane
solvent

What has happened?

1 Find out what the word 'halogen' means

2 Look at the picture at the top of the opposite page. What does it tell you about the melting points of the halogens as you go down the group?

3 Look at the pictures in the middle of the opposite page. What would you eventually expect to happen to the indicator containing iodine solution?

4 Write equations for the reactions of
  a bromine and water
  b iodine and sodium hydroxide solution.

5 Why would it be dangerous to flush battery acid down a drain using a household bleach?

6 State what you would observe and write equations for the reactions (if any) if the experiments in the photos above were carried out using
  a potassium iodide (KI) and chlorine
  b potassium iodide (KI) and bromine
  c potassium chloride and bromine

7 Write down as many similarities as you can find between the elements chlorine and bromine.

8 In what ways are the halogens different to the alkali metals?

2.7   *Patterns in the middle: Group 4*

Physical patterns

Group 4 is a 'family' of elements in the middle of the Periodic Table. The first element in the group, carbon, is found naturally in two different forms – diamond and graphite. The table shows that the elements in this group have a mixture of metallic and non-metallic properties. If you look at the position of the group in the Periodic Table this is not as surprising as it might at first seem. Can you suggest a reason for it?

Chemical patterns – the oxides

You have already seen (2.2) that you can find out about the chemical nature of an element by looking at the chemical properties of its oxide. Metals form basic oxides and non-metals, such as carbon, form acidic oxides. But elements in Group 4 have more than one oxide. Carbon, for example, forms carbon dioxide, CO_2, *and* (the less stable) carbon monoxide, CO. For simplicity you can study the more representative oxide of each element – which in the case of carbon is carbon dioxide.

The acidic nature of carbon dioxide can be shown by ▶ its reaction with the alkaline solutions of metal hydroxides such as calcium hydroxide, $Ca(OH)_2$ – limewater. Carbon dioxide reacts with limewater to produce a white cloudy precipitate of calcium carbonate.

Calcium hydroxide → calcium carbonate + water
+ carbon dioxide   + carbon dioxide
$$Ca(OH)_2 + CO_2 \rightarrow CaCO_3 + H_2O + CO_2$$

Many of the Group 4 oxides are insoluble in water so it is not possible to find out if they form acidic or basic solutions. Silicon dioxide, SiO_2, for example, is the main ingredient of sand – and you know that sand isn't soluble! However, some acidic oxides will react with some basic oxides. Sodium is a metallic element from Group 1 and sodium oxide, Na_2O, is therefore a basic oxide. This reacts with SiO_2 to form sodium silicate, Na_2SiO_3.

$$Na_2O + SiO_2 \rightarrow Na_2SiO_3$$

This shows that SiO_2 is an acidic oxide – so silicon behaves chemically as a non-metal like carbon.

▌ *SiO_2 reacts with lead oxide, PbO, to form lead silicate which is used in cut glass. What type of oxide is PbO?*

Although lead oxide, PbO, is a basic oxide when it reacts with SiO_2, it also reacts with a metal hydroxide such as sodium hydroxide. This shows it can also react as an acidic oxide, like carbon dioxide. Metal oxides like lead oxide which have the properties of both basic and acidic oxides are called **amphoteric oxides**.

Element	Appearance	Electrical conductivity	Ductility
C Carbon	graphite: shiny black solid	good	poor
	diamond: clear solid		
Si Silicon	shiny grey solid	semi-conductor	poor
Pb Lead	shiny grey-blue solid	good	good

The reaction of CO_2 with limewater (calcium hydroxide solution) produces a white cloudy precipitate. This reaction is used as a test for CO_2.

Sodium silicate or water glass is used to make crystal gardens.

Metallic versus non-metallic character

When atoms of elements in Groups 1 to 8 are involved in chemical reactions they try to obtain noble gas electronic structures (*see 2.4 and 2.5*). They try to fill their shells – the first shell can hold 2 electrons and the other shells 8 electrons each. The way each atom does this depends on the number of electrons in this outer shell.

Atoms with less than 4 electrons in their outer shell *lose* these electrons. This is a characteristic reaction of a *metal*. Atoms with more than 4 electrons in their outer shell *gain* the electrons from metal atoms they are reacting with. This is a characteristic reaction of a *non-metal*. Look at what happens to metallic magnesium atoms and non-metallic oxygen atoms when they combine to form magnesium oxide. ▶

Atoms of non-metals can also achieve full shells in another way. They can *share* electrons with other non-metal atoms. The diagram shows you how nitrogen and chlorine atoms share electrons to form nitrogen chloride. ▼

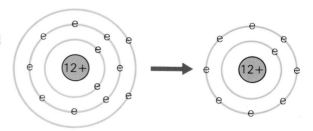

The Mg atom, electronic structure 2,8,2 loses 2 electrons . . .

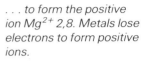

. . . to form the positive ion Mg^{2+} 2,8. Metals lose electrons to form positive ions.

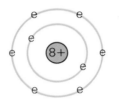

The O atom, electronic structure 2,6 gains the 2 electrons lost by the Mg atom . . .

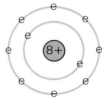

. . . to form the negative ion O^{2-} 2,8. Non-metals gain electrons to form negative ions.

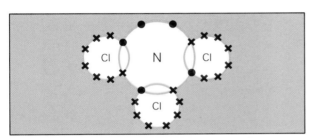

By sharing electrons (● and X), nitrogen and chlorine can achieve 8 electrons in their outer shells.

1 Look at the table on the opposite page. What physical properties of graphite suggest it is **a** a metal **b** a non-metal?

2 Why would you expect the chemical properties of diamond and graphite to be identical even though their physical properties are different?

3 What do the chemical properties of the oxides show you about the metallic character of the elements as you go down Group 4?

4 Look at the elements in the table below.

Element	Li	S	F	Ca	Al
Atomic number	3	16	9	20	13

Which would you expect to behave as metals and which as non-metals?

5 The **valency** of an element is the number of electrons lost, gained or shared when it reacts with other elements. What is the valency of each of the elements in question 4?

Changes in Group 4

The position of an element in the Periodic Table is given by its number of electrons – its **atomic number**. The group shows the number of electrons in the outer shell of each element. So all elements in Group 4 have 4 electrons in their outer shell. Because of this you might think these elements could equally lose, gain or share their 4 outer electrons to get full shells. However, they rarely gain electrons and other factors such as the size of atoms make a difference as to whether they lose or share (*see 2.5*).

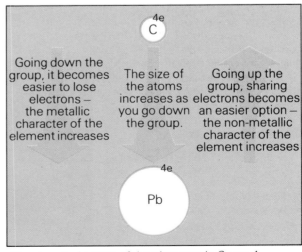

The chemical nature of the elements in Group 4 changes as you go up and down the group.

6 Which element would you expect to be more metallic – nitrogen or antimony? Give a reason for your answer.

2.8 *Patterns in the reactions of metals*

Reactions with water

The majority of elements in the Periodic Table are metals. You have already seen patterns in the family of metallic elements in Group 1 (*see 2.5*). You can build up a general pattern for other metals in the same way by looking at different reactions. The picture shows you the reactions of three different metals with cold water.

When calcium reacts with cold water an alkaline solution containing calcium hydroxide is formed and hydrogen gas is released.

$$Ca + 2H_2O \rightarrow Ca(OH)_2 + H_2$$

How does this reaction compare with the reactions of the Group 1 metals with water?

Calcium Magnesium Copper

There is a large difference in the reactivity of these metals with water. Which metal is the most reactive?

Reaction with acids

Some metals react with acids such as hydrochloric (HCl) and sulphuric (H_2SO_4). The reaction produces hydrogen and a solution containing a **salt.** The salt formed depends on the type of acid. Hydrochloric acid produces salts called *chlorides* and sulphuric acid produces salts called *sulphates.* For example, magnesium forms magnesium chloride when reacting with hydrochloric acid but magnesium sulphate when reacting with sulphuric acid. The equations for the reactions are:

$$Mg + 2HCl \rightarrow MgCl_2 + H_2$$
$$Mg + H_2SO_4 \rightarrow MgSO_4 + H_2$$

The equations for the reactions of iron with the two acids are very similar except that the salts formed are iron chloride ($FeCl_2$) and iron sulphate ($FeSO_4$).

Magnesium Iron Copper

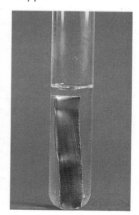

You can also obtain an order of reactivity by reacting metals with acids.

Displacement reactions

A more reactive metal will displace a less reactive metal from a solution of its salt. For example, if a piece of magnesium is placed in copper sulphate solution it will displace copper from the solution because magnesium is more reactive than copper. The surface of the more reactive metal (magnesium) becomes coated in the less reactive metal (copper):

$$Mg + CuSO_4 \rightarrow MgSO_4 + Cu$$

It's easy to coat some metals with copper using displacement reactions, but electroplating like this gives longer lasting coatings.

Simple cells

A battery or simple cell contains two metals of different reactivity in a conducting solution – an **electrolyte**. You can measure the energy output of the cell by a voltmeter connected to the two metal plates or electrodes, as shown here. The difference in reactivity between the magnesium and copper is much greater than the difference in reactivity between the iron and the copper.

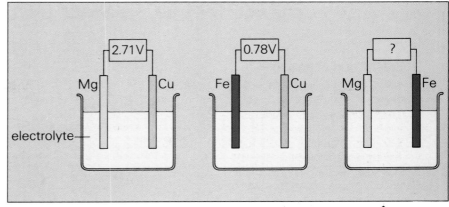

What does this show you about the difference in reactivity between two metals and the size of the voltmeter reading?

The reactivity series

You can order metals in a 'league table' of reactivity called the reactivity series. This is based on their reactions with other chemicals such as water and acids as well as their displacement reactions and the energy output of simple cells. The higher a metal's position in the league table, the more reactive it is. The diagram shows you the position of some metals in the table. It can also help you to predict the voltage output of a simple cell. What do you think the voltmeter reading will be in the cell in the diagram above using magnesium (Mg) and iron (Fe) electrodes?

1 Why do you think lithium batteries do not use electrolytes containing water?

2 Look at the first picture. What do you notice about the reactivity of the Group 2 metals (Mg and Ca) as you go down the group? Is this similar to the pattern found in Group 1?

3 Write equations for the reaction of iron with hydrochloric and sulphuric acids.

4 Which metals in the reactivity series on the right will react with acids but not displace magnesium from magnesium sulphate solution?

5 Why do you think copper is an ideal metal to use in making coins?

6 **a** A simple cell gives a voltage output of 0.32 volts. What two metals could have been used as electrodes?
b What would be the voltage output of a simple cell that used the same metal as both electrodes?

7 Chemical reactions involve transfer of electrons. Why do you think alkali metals like lithium give high readings of voltage compared with other metals?

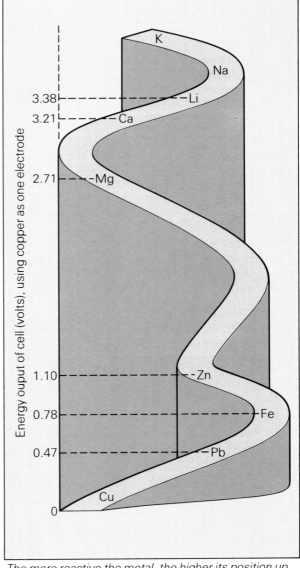

The more reactive the metal, the higher its position up the slope.

YOU CAN READ MORE ABOUT REACTIVITY SERIES ON SPREAD 4.8

2.9 Patterns across a period

A physical changeover

A period is a horizontal row of elements in the Periodic Table. Each period contains a different number of elements. The 1st period only contains two elements – hydrogen and helium – and the 2nd and 3rd periods contain eight elements each. Apart from the first and last periods, each one starts with an alkali metal and finishes with a noble gas.

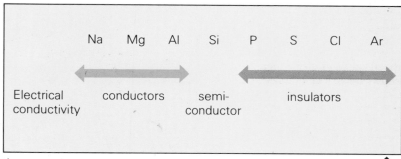

Na   Mg   Al   Si   P   S   Cl   Ar

Electrical conductivity ← conductors → semi-conductor ← insulators →

As you go from Group 1 to Group 8 across the Periodic Table there is a changeover from metallic to non-metallic properties. Where does the changeover occur in the 3rd period, shown here?

A chemical changeover

There seems to be a change in the physical properties of the elements at silicon – elements before this behave as metals and after as non-metals. You can determine whether there is also a change in their chemical properties by looking at the reactions of the oxides. Remember metals form oxides and hydroxides that react with acids. Non-metals form oxides that react with alkalis.

Aluminium is coated with a thin layer of aluminium oxide, Al_2O_3. Look at the pictures. How do they show that the changeover in chemical properties from metals to non-metals in this period occurs at aluminium?

If you cook rhubarb or make jam in an aluminium pan, the surface layer is removed. The acids released by cooking react with the Al_2O_3 as well as attacking the metal.

Reactivity with water

The first element in the period, sodium, reacts violently with cold water, whilst the last element, argon, is completely unreactive with water – and with all other substances! Although this might seem to indicate that the reactivity decreases as you go from Na to Ar, the pictures show you that there is no clear pattern across the whole period. Can you suggest why this is not entirely unexpected?

CAUTION:
Do not use on aluminium or chromium. Avoid contact with paintwork and floor covering. Refer to oven manufacturers's instructions, particularly for cleaning glass doors.

Pressurised container. Protect from sunlight and do not expose to temperatures exceeding 50°C. Do not pierce or burn even after use. Do not spray on a naked flame or any incandescent material.

IRRITANT. CONTAINS CAUSTIC SODIUM HYDROXIDE IRRITATING TO EYES AND SKIN. IN CASE OF CONTACT WITH EYES RINSE

Many kitchen cleaners are not suitable for cleaning aluminium. The alkalis in the cleaners react with the Al_2O_3 before reacting with the metal.

Magnesium reacts with steam to produce magnesium oxide, MgO, and hydrogen.

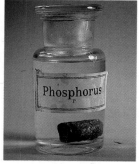

Phosphorus

Phosphorus can set fire spontaneously in air but can safely be stored in water.

Chlorine reacts with water forming a germicide used in swimming baths.

Formula of hydride	NaH	MgH$_2$	AlH$_3$	SiH$_4$	PH$_3$	H$_2$S	HCl
Common name	sodium hydride	magnesium hydride	alane	silane	phosphine	hydrogen sulphide	hydrogen chloride
Valency (V) of element in the period	1	2	3	4	3	2	1

The formula of the hydrides depends on the valencies of the elements

$V = 2 \quad V = 1$
Mg   H , crossing over the valencies gives the simplest formula MgH$_2$ (the number 1 is omitted). When valencies are greater than 1, you might have to divide by the smallest valency to find the simplest formula which is based on whole numbers.

$V = 2 \quad V = 2$
Mg   O , crossing over the valencies and dividing by 2 gives the simplest formula MgO.

$V = 3 \quad V = 2$
B   O , crossing over the valencies gives B$_2$O$_3$. You don't divide by the smallest valency, 2, since this doesn't give whole numbers.

Patterns in the formulae of hydrides

When an element combines with hydrogen, it forms a hybride. Look at the table, showing you the formulae of the hydrides across the 3rd short period. You can see that the number of atoms of hydrogen joining with one atom of Mg and S is the same. In each case 2 atoms of hydrogen join with 1 atom of each Mg or S. The numbers give us information about the **valency** of an atom (*see 2.7*). In this example, the valancy of hydrogen is 1; the valency of magnesium and sulphur is 2. Valencies are useful in helping you to work out the simplest formula of a compound. If you look at magnesium hydride to see how its formula has been worked out, you will see that the valencies of magnesium and hydrogen have been *crossed over*. Has the same method been used to obtain the formula of hydrogen sulphide?

Valency and atomic structure

As you go along the period from Na to Ar, the atomic number and hence the number of electrons increases by one. The electronic structure of the atoms shows that the number of electrons in the outer shell also increases by one. When atoms of elements react they achieve full electronic structures by gaining, losing or sharing electrons (*see 2.7*). The diagram below shows how the atoms of elements in the 3rd period do this.

Atomic number	Na 11	Mg 12	Al 13	Si 14	P 15	S 16	Cl 17	Ar 18
Electronic structure	2,8,1	2,8,2	2,8,3	2,8,4	2,8,5	2,8,6	2,8,7	2,8,8
Atom achieves noble gas electronic structure by ...	losing electrons (Al sometimes shares)			sharing electrons		gaining or sharing electrons		
No. of electrons lost, gained or shared	1	2	3	4	3	2	1	

Can you see a connection between the valency and the number of electrons lost, gained or shared?

1 Look at the Periodic Table on 2.1.
  a How many elements are there in the 4th, 5th and 6th periods?
  b How many elements will have to be made in the 7th period before a noble gas is made?

2 Why is the valency of argon zero? What do you think is the main chemical characteristic of the noble gas elements?

3 Use the valencies above to deduce the formulae of sodium oxide, aluminium oxide and silicon oxide.

4 Use the Periodic Table to deduce the valencies of nitrogen and fluorine. What is the formula of the compound formed by the combination of these elements?

5 Element X reacts with element Y to form XY$_3$. Element Z reacts with Y to form ZY$_2$. What is the formula of the compound formed between X and Z?

6 Why does the way in which atoms achieve a noble gas electronic structure match the finding that the metallic character of elements decreases across the 3rd short period?

2.10 Patterns in forming salts

Acids

Acids are a very important group of chemicals. The vinegar that you may put on your fish and chips contains ethanoic acid. Hydrochloric acid is used in your stomach to help you digest your food. Hydrochloric acid is also used by chemists as an acid in the laboratory along with sulphuric and nitric acids. Like all acids, their dilute solutions in water have a pH less than 7 and they have the same effect on indicators such as turning blue litmus paper red (*see 2.2*). They also react with compounds called bases.

Name of acid	Formula of acid
hydrochloric	HCl
sulphuric	H_2SO_4
nitric	HNO_3
ethanoic	$HOOCCH_3$

The table shows you the formulae of the common laboratory acids. What element is common to all the acids?

Bases

Bases are substances that cancel out or neutralise acids. This means the base reacts with the acid and removes its acidic properties. The diagrams show you examples of acids being neutralised by bases. Bases which dissolve in water are given a special name – **alkalis**. Alkalis have a pH greater than 7 and turn red litmus paper blue.

What happens on neutralisation?

When an **acid** reacts with a **base**, a **salt** and **other products** are formed.

Bases determine the other products . . .
The picture below shows you what is formed when the *same* acid is added to *different* bases. Note that the type of salt is the *same* but the other products are *different*.

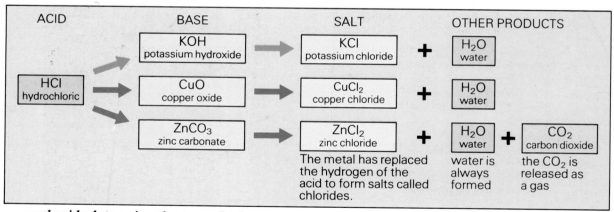

. . . and acids determine the type of salt
When the *same* base is added to *different* acids, note how the type of salt is *different* but the other product of the reaction is the *same*.

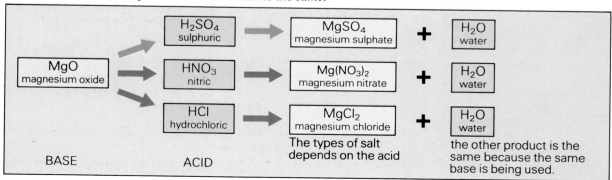

42

Making salts

When a salt is made from an acid and a base it is important to make sure that all the acid has been neutralised by the base. The method you should use to prepare the base depends on the solubility of the base in water.

Insoluble base: The only way to be sure that all the acid has been neutralised is to use more base than is needed. This is called using *excess base*.

Excess of an insoluble base such as copper carbonate (CuCO₃) is added to neutralise all the sulphuric acid . . .

. . .The excess base is filtered off and the copper sulphate solution collected in an evaporating basin . . .

*. . . **Some** of the water is slowly evaporated. Copper sulphate crystals are formed when the remaining solution is left to cool. This can be collected and dried on filter paper.*

Alkali (soluble base): It is not possible to filter off an excess of a soluble base, so another way has to be found! The only way to be sure that all the acid has been used up is to use *exactly* the right amount of base. At this point the mixture will be neutral – so a suitable indicator can be used.

An indicator such as phenolphthalein is added to the acid to show when it has been neutralised.

1 Magnesium hydroxide is used to cure acid indigestion. What salt does it produce in your stomach?

2 Acid rain contains a mixture of nitric and sulphuric acids. What is formed when it corrodes buildings or statues made of limestone (calcium carbonate)?

3 Hydrogencarbonates give the same 'other products' as carbonates. What is formed when sodium hydrogencarbonate reacts with nitric acid?

4 Potassium nitrate is used to make fireworks. Suggest a suitable acid and base from which it can be made. Why should the potassium nitrate solution produced not be evaporated to dryness to obtain crystals?

5 Look at the preparation of copper sulphate.
  a How would you know when all the acid had been used up?
  b Why is it better to stir the mixture of acid and base?

6 Look at the preparation of sodium chloride.
  a What colour is the phenolphthalein in the acid?
  b What colour would it turn if one drop of excess alkali were added?
  c Why is the maximum yield of sodium chloride not obtained by evaporating part of the water?

7 Which of the two methods for preparing salt would you use to prepare
  a KNO_3 from KOH and HNO_3
  b $ZnCl_2$ from ZnO and HCl?

2.11 Looking at neutralisation

That effervescent feeling

Many people prefer to take tablets such as aspirin or paracetamol in soluble form rather than having to swallow them. Manufacturers add an 'effervescent base' to make these soluble tablets. This means they add a base which reacts with an acid to produce a gas. The tablet also contains an acid in solid form such as ascorbic acid (Vitamin C) or citric acid found in citric fruits. When the tablet is added to water, carbon dioxide is produced. This disperses the less soluble particles evenly throughout the water.

Soluble tablets like soluble aspirin contain an acid and an 'effervescent base' such as sodium carbonate or sodium hydrogencarbonate.

Products when bases react with acids

Base	'Active' part	Water H_2O	Carbon dioxide CO_2
metal oxide	oxide ion O^{2-}	✓	✗
metal	hydroxide OH^-	✓	✗
metal carbonate	carbonate ion CO_3^{2-}	✓	✓
metal hydrogen-carbonate	hydrogen-carbonate HCO_3^-	✓	✓

The basic ingredient

When deciding which base to use, the manufacturers of soluble tablets use the fact that *any* metal carbonate or hydrogencarbonate will react with *any* acid to produce water and carbon dioxide. The active part of the base is the carbonate ion, CO_3^{2-}, or hydrogencarbonate ion, HCO_3^-. Other bases such as metal oxides and hydroxides have active parts as the table shows. The fact that the product depends on the 'active' part of the bases and not the acid suggests that in *all* acids the same particle is reacting with the base.

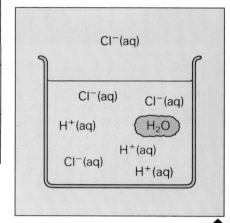

Hydrochloric acid is fully dissociated into H^+ (aq) ions and chloride ions, Cl^- (aq) in water.

The active ingredient in acids

In a tablet containing an acid and a base such as a metal carbonate, the acid and base don't react until they have been added to water. The particle in the acid responsible for its properties only exists when the acid has been dissolved in water. When an acid molecule is added to water, it breaks up or *dissociates* into ions. The two diagrams show you what happens when hydrochloric acid (HCl) and ethanoic acid (CH_3COOH) are added to water. The (aq) after each ion means **aqueous**. This tells you the ion is surrounded by a number of water molecules (think of *aquatic, aquarium*!). The ion is said to be **hydrated**. The particle common to both acids is the hydrated hydrogen ion, H^+ (aq). The strength of the acid depends on the concentration of H^+ (aq) ions in the solution.

How do the diagrams explain why hydrochloric acid is a strong acid but ethanoic acid is weak?

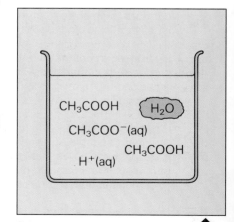

Ethanoic acid, CH_3COOH, is only partly dissociated into H^+ (aq) ions and ethanoate ions, CH_3COO^- (aq) in water.

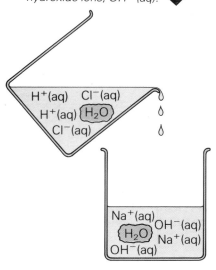

Sodium hydroxide solution is fully dissociated into positive sodium ions, Na⁺ (aq) and negative hydroxide ions, OH⁻ (aq).

Neutralisation

If a soluble base or alkali such as a Group 1 metal hydroxide, MOH, is dissolved in water it dissociates into positive ions, M^+ (aq), and negative hydroxide ions, OH^- (aq). The diagram below shows what happens when hydrochloric acid is added to sodium hydroxide solution.

The reaction between the sodium hydroxide and the hydrochloric acid can be represented by the 'active' part of the acid and the 'active' part of the base. The 'active' part of the acid is *always* H^+ (aq) and in this example the 'active' part of the base is OH^- (aq). The equation representing this reaction now becomes:

hydrated hydrogen ions + hydrated hydroxide ions → water
or $\quad H^+$ (aq) + OH^- (aq) $\quad$ → H_2O.

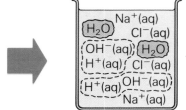

When hydrochloric acid is added, the H^+ (aq) ions and OH^- (aq) ions react to form . . .

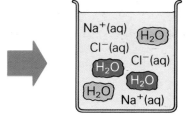

. . . water. The Na^+ (aq) and Cl^- (aq) ions remain as a solution of sodium chloride. The salt has not taken part in the reaction – it is a chemical 'leftover'.

This is called an *ionic* equation. Note that the product is the same as that in the table opposite. For an insoluble base some of the base, however small, will actually dissolve in the water. This means an insoluble metal carbonate will always have a small part of the 'active' carbonate ion in solution as CO_3^{2-} (aq). This will react with any H^+ (aq) ions in solution to give the products shown in the table opposite. As it reacts, more carbonate dissolves.

$$CO_3^{2-} \text{ (aq)} + 2H^+ \text{ (aq)} \rightarrow H_2O + CO_2.$$

Proton donors and acceptors

The hydrogen ion, H^+, is formed by a hydrogen atom losing an electron.

$$H - e \rightarrow H^+$$

The diagram shows that a hydrogen ion is a proton.

Since all acids give their protons to bases when they are neutralised by them, they are called **proton donors**. Why do you think bases are called **proton acceptors**?

When a hydrogen atom loses an electron, it forms a proton.

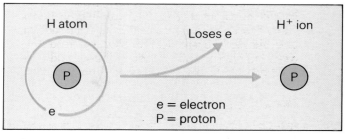

$\boxed{1}$ Why do you think Vitamin C and citric acid are commonly used in soluble medicine tablets?

$\boxed{2}$ What other factors does a manufacturer need to consider when choosing a metal carbonate for a soluble tablet?

$\boxed{3}$ Nitric acid produces the nitrate ion, NO_3^-, and sulphuric acid the sulphate ion, SO_4^{2-}, when dissolved in water. They are both strong acids. Draw models to show what happens when they dissolve in water.

$\boxed{4}$ Draw a model similar to the one at the top of the page to explain what happens when sulphuric acid is added to copper carbonate ($Cu^{2+}CO_3^{2-}$).

$\boxed{5}$ Write an ionic equation for the reaction between
a potassium hydrogencarbonate and nitric acid
b magnesium oxide and hydrochloric acid.

$\boxed{6}$ Ammonia (NH_3) is a base and reacts with an acid to form the ammonium ion (NH_4^+). Write an ionic equation for its reaction with an acid.

45

What happens in solutions?

Positive ions		Negative ions		
+1	K^+ potassium Na^+ sodium	−1	NO_3^- nitrate OH^- hydroxide Cl^- chloride	
+2	Mg^{2+} magnesium Pb^{2+} lead	−2	O^{2-} oxide SO_4^{2-} sulphate CO_3^{2-} carbonate	
+3	Al^{3+} aluminium			
Metals form positive ions		**Non-metals** (separately or in groups) **usually form negative ions**		

Charged ions, but neutral compounds

Positive or negative ions don't occur on their own. If they did the milk or toothpaste would be electrically charged and you'd get an electric shock! There are always oppositely charged ions present; these cancel the charges out. In a solid, the oppositely charged ions are packed closely together and form strong forces of attraction called **ionic bonds** (*see 3.7*). Some toothpastes contain solid aluminium hydroxide as an abrasive to help to remove plaque. In aluminium hydroxide there are three hydroxide ions (OH^-) for every aluminium ion (Al^{3+}), so the charges cancel out.

Soluble or insoluble?

Most toothpastes contain about 20% water by weight (so that the paste can be squeezed easily out of the tube!) The fluoride is usually provided by a compound such as sodium fluoride, and this dissolves in the water. If aluminium hydroxide is to act effectively as an abrasive it is important that it does *not* dissolve. Whether an ionic compound dissolves in water depends on the type of ions present. Some combinations of positive and negative ions are more soluble in water than others. Use these solubility rules when you want to find out if an ionic compound is soluble.

Ions do it their way!

You may drink milk because it contains calcium, and use toothpaste that contains fluoride because both are good for your teeth. But as pure elements fluorine and calcium are highly reactive and would do you more harm than good. However when they are present as **ions** – calcium ions and fluoride ions – they can help to keep your bones and teeth healthy. So, ions can behave differently to the elements from which they are formed – they have their own properties, such as an ability to dissolve in water. Some common ions and their respective charges are shown here.

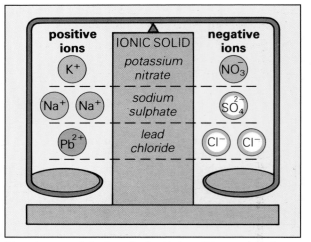

The charges of the ions in the ionic solid cancel each other – they balance!

SOLUBILITY RULES

1. Any solid is **soluble** if it contains
   - sodium ions ⎫
   - potassium ions ⎬ See ◯ above
   - nitrate ions ⎭
   - chloride ions – *except silver or lead chloride*
   - sulphate ions – *except calcium, barium or lead sulphate*

2. Any solid is **insoluble** if it contains
   - oxide ions ⎫
   - hydroxide ions ⎬ *except for sodium or potassium compounds.*
   - carbonate ions ⎭

What happens on dissolving?

If an ionic compound is water-soluble, it dissolves in water to form a solution containing **aqueous** (dissolved) **ions**. When sodium chloride dissolves in water it forms a solution containing aqueous sodium ions, $Na^+(aq)$, and aqueous chloride ions, $Cl^-(aq)$.

Reversing the process

If two aqueous solutions containing free ions are mixed, they can immediately produce an insoluble solid in the mixture. The insoluble solid is called a **precipitate**.

Precipitation is a chemical reaction that sometimes occurs when two solutions of ions are mixed. The word equation for the reaction shown below can be written

Sodium carbonate + Magnesium sulphate → Sodium sulphate + Magnesium carbonate (↓)

The downward arrow indicates that this product is formed as a precipitate.

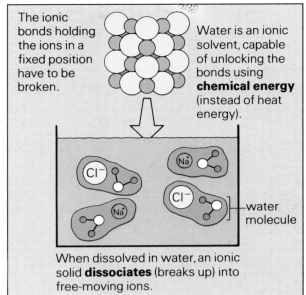

The ionic bonds holding the ions in a fixed position have to be broken.

Water is an ionic solvent, capable of unlocking the bonds using **chemical energy** (instead of heat energy).

water molecule

When dissolved in water, an ionic solid **dissociates** (breaks up) into free-moving ions.

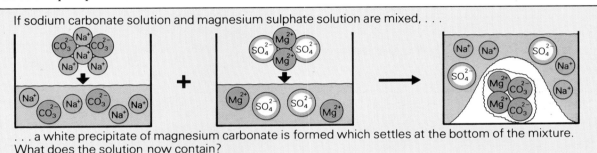

If sodium carbonate solution and magnesium sulphate solution are mixed, . . .

. . . a white precipitate of magnesium carbonate is formed which settles at the bottom of the mixture. What does the solution now contain?

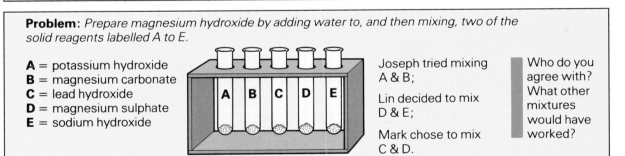

Problem: *Prepare magnesium hydroxide by adding water to, and then mixing, two of the solid reagents labelled A to E.*

A = potassium hydroxide
B = magnesium carbonate
C = lead hydroxide
D = magnesium sulphate
E = sodium hydroxide

Joseph tried mixing A & B;

Lin decided to mix D & E;

Mark chose to mix C & D.

Who do you agree with? What other mixtures would have worked?

---

1 Draw the ions present in:
 a calcium nitrate; **b** lead hydroxide.

2 Use the solubility rules to explain why:
 a aluminium hydroxide is insoluble;
 b sodium fluoride is soluble.

3 If you suspected tap-water from old lead pipes was contaminated with lead ions what solution could you add to the tap-water to identify the lead? Why?

4 Refer back to spread 1.4 and explain the difference between a molecule and an ionic compound dissolving.

5 **a** Suggest two solutions you could mix to obtain a precipitate of aluminium hydroxide.
 b What technique would you use to separate the precipitate from the rest of the mixture?

6 **a** Name the precipitate formed by mixing solutions of sodium sulphate to barium chloride
 b What is present in solution afterwards?

3.1 Changing state

What a state!

These three photographs show changes in the properties of a common substance. What changes in the properties can you see that have taken place? Why do you think the substance has changed in this way?

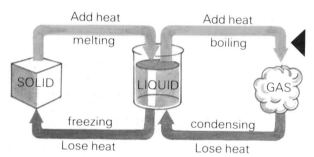

Different states

The boiling kettle and the frozen pondwater above show how the same substance, water, can be changed by heating and cooling. Steam and ice are clearly different from the liquid you see when you turn on a tap. By changing the temperature of water it can become a solid (ice) or a gas (steam).

Solids, liquids and gases are called the **three states of matter**. Ice, water and steam are all different states of the same substance – water. The change from one state to another can be reversed: water freezes to ice and ice can melt back to water.

Getting things moving

The particles which make up a solid are very close to each other and do not move away from their fixed position as they are held by other particles around them. When a solid is heated, its particles gain energy, causing them to break free from their fixed position and begin to move around. This causes solids to melt into liquids. The temperature at which this happens is called the **melting point**.

By making the particles of a substance move about more rapidly, solids become liquids and liquids become gases. When water is heated its particles gain enough energy to escape from the liquid into the air. This happens slowly when water is heated by the sun and **evaporates** from the pavement after a shower of rain. It can happen quickly when water is heated until it boils. When a substance boils, bubbles of gas form inside the liquid and rise to the surface. The temperature at which this happens is called the **boiling point**. Evaporation can happen below the boiling point.

In a solid the particles are very close and they do not move away from their fixed position.

In a liquid the particles are further apart. They have more energy and move.

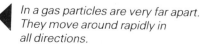

In a gas particles are very far apart. They move around rapidly in all directions.

Moving about . . .

You may be watching television or doing homework in one room but you can often smell something cooking in the kitchen. This is because gas particles from the food spread out from the kitchen to other parts of your home. This movement of gas particles from one place to another is called **diffusion**. Diffusion can also take place in liquids such as when coffee particles spread out in water in a cup of instant coffee. However, diffusion in liquids is much slower than diffusion in gases.

. . . at different speeds

Gas particles move at different speeds. They also move about very fast – a speed of 400 metres every second is not unusual. But our own experience from such things as smells moving about the home tells us that they appear to move much more slowly. This is because gas particles are constantly getting in one another's way. The gas particles move more slowly because they are constantly colliding with each other. (Imagine you and your friends trying to get into a classroom when everybody else is trying to get out.) The gas particles from the food are constantly colliding with each other and with other gas particles already present in the air. The experiment below helps you to compare the speeds at which two gases diffuse.

The diffusion of carbon dioxide in air is often used to create special effects.

The white band of ammonium chloride is formed nearer to the hydrogen chloride than the ammonia.

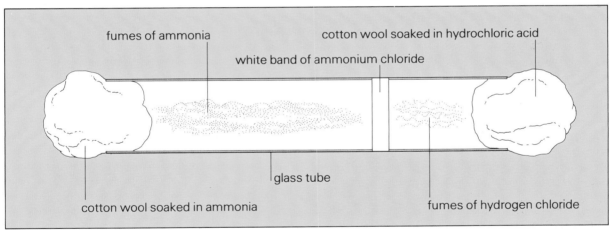

fumes of ammonia

cotton wool soaked in hydrochloric acid

white band of ammonium chloride

glass tube

cotton wool soaked in ammonia

fumes of hydrogen chloride

---

1 Why does diffusion in liquids take place more slowly than diffusion in gases?

2 Why do solids not diffuse?

3 Give two other examples of diffusion of gases and liquids found in the home.

4 A vacuum contains no air. Can you suggest why a gas diffuses faster in a vacuum than in air?

5 Do you think gas particles will diffuse faster or slower at higher temperatures? Give reasons for your answer.

6 Look at the position of the white band formed when the ammonia meets the hydrogen chloride. Which gas diffuses faster. Can you suggest a reason?

3.2 Atomic structure

Early models

The idea that matter is made up of tiny particles is not new. Almost 2500 years ago, the Greek philosopher Epicurus suggested that it would not be possible to go on dividing a piece of matter indefinitely. In 1808 a Manchester school teacher, John Dalton, resurrected the age-old idea of the Greeks. He imagined different elements to be made of different types of very small indestructible spheres. He called these spheres **atoms** after the Greek word *atomos* which means *indivisible*.

Dalton imagined all the atoms of one element to be the same size and mass. When atoms combined to form compounds, he believed they remained unchanged. ▼

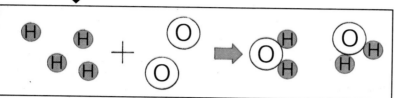

The Greeks imagined that atoms had different shapes and sizes – and that some atoms had 'hooks'. ▼

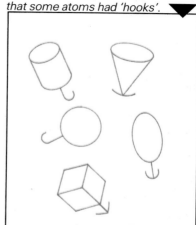

The model falls apart!

Towards the end of the nineteenth century, other particles were discovered which came from atoms. The atom was not after all indivisible. These particles were called **sub-atomic particles**. J.J. Thomson was the first person to discover a sub-atomic particle. The year was 1897 and he called it the **electron** after the Greek word *elecktra* which means *charge*.

The electron has a very small mass compared to the rest of the atom. It also has a negative charge (in contrast to the uncharged atom).

Positive 'drops' of matter with same mass as atoms had been discovered by Goldstein in 1886.

These discoveries led J.J. Thomson to propose a new model for the atom

Thomson imagined the atom as a **cloud of positive charge** with **negative electrons** spread throughout like 'plums in a pudding'

The proof of the pudding ..

In 1911, Ernest Rutherford, a New Zealand scientist working at Manchester University, decided to test Thomson's model experimentally. It was well known that *like charges repel one another* – the greater the concentration of charge, the greater the repulsion. Rutherford decided to use positive particles, called α **(alpha)** particles as high speed 'bullets' which would be repelled by the positive cloud.

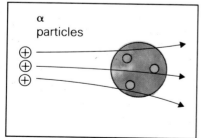

If Thomson was correct, positive 'bullets' would pass through with slight deflections due to the atom's widespread positive cloud.

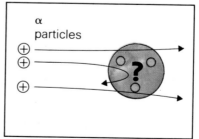

Rutherford was surprised – the deflections were much larger than expected. Some 'bullets' even deflected straight back!

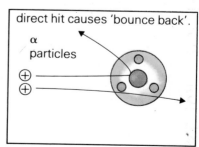

*Rutherford realised there must be a high concentration of positive charge just at the **centre** of the atom.*

50

Classifying atoms

Rutherford was able to show that the positive charge at the centre of the atom was due to positively charged particles. He called these particles **protons**. The charge on the proton is *equal* in size but *opposite* to the negative charge on the electron – however the proton is about 2000 times heavier than the electron.

All the atoms of one element have the *same number* of protons – this number is very important because it tells us which **element** an atom belongs to. The number of protons in an atom of an element is called its **atomic number**. Since an atom is electrically neutral (it has no overall charge) *the number of protons is always equal to the number of electrons.*

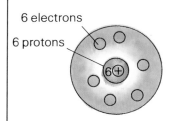

All carbon atoms have 6 protons in the nucleus and 6 electrons. It has an atomic number of 6.

All fluorine atoms have 9 protons in the nucleus and 9 electrons.
What is its atomic number?

The element sodium, Na, can be written

Mass N° → **23**
Atomic N° → **11** **Na**

It has 11 protons, 11 electrons and 12 neutrons.
The atomic structure of sodium is

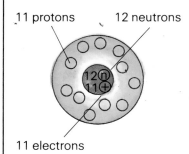

11 protons   12 neutrons

11 electrons

The mass of atoms

Although most atoms of an element have the same mass, in 1918 Aston found that a few atoms of an element had different mass. Since these atoms reacted *chemically* in *the same* way as normal atoms, they must have the *same atomic number* (which means they each have the same number of protons). So, what was causing the difference in the mass?

Chadwick answered this in 1932 when he discovered neutral particles with the same mass as protons. They were called **neutrons** and (like protons) they were found in the **nucleus** of the atom. To identify an atom fully, a number was needed from which the number of neutrons could be found. This number is called the **mass number**.

Mass number = Number of protons + Number of neutrons

An atom of a particular element must still have the same number of protons and electrons but it may have various numbers of neutrons. Atoms with the same number of protons and electrons but different numbers of neutrons are called isotopes. **Isotopes** are *chemically the same* as the normal atoms of an element, but have a *different mass number*.

So far, so good – but Rutherford's model (though helpful) is not the most accurate atomic model. To find out more see spread 3.4.

1   In what ways were the Greeks' ideas the same or different to Dalton's?

2   How many positive units of charge must there be in Thomson's model of an atom shown opposite?

3   Draw Rutherford's model of the atom showing the path of an *undeflected* particle.

4   How does Rutherford's model of the atom explain the fact that only a few particles were deflected backwards?

5   Complete the following Table

Particle	Relative Mass	Relative Charge
electron	?	−1
proton	1	?
neutron	?	?

6   Phosphorus has 2 isotopes $^{31}_{15}P$ and $^{30}_{15}P$
   a Explain why they are isotopes.
   b What is the atomic number and mass number of each isotope?
   c Work out the number of protons, neutrons and electrons in each isotope.

3.3 Molecules

Atoms – the 'master builders'

Everything on earth, including you, is made up of tiny particles called **atoms**. Although there are millions of different substances on Earth, they are made from only about 90 different types of atoms. Atoms are the 'master builders', capable of joining together in many different combinations to produce the world you live in.

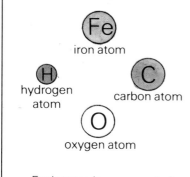

iron atom

hydrogen atom

carbon atom

oxygen atom

Each atom is represented by a name and a symbol

Iron is an *element*

If a substance contains only one type of atom it is called an **element**. Most elements are metals but a few are non-metals.

Sand (silicon oxide) is a *compound* containing the atoms silicon and oxygen

Some atoms of elements can join together to form new substances. If a substance contains different types of atoms joined together it is called a **compound**.

Combining atoms

The simplest combination of atoms is a small group or cluster called **molecules**. These are formed by atoms of non-metal elements joining together. The atoms in a molecule are held together by strong forces of attraction. The forces of attraction between atoms are called **bonds**. This diagram shows how different atoms are held together by the strong forces of attraction (strong bonds) inside molecules.

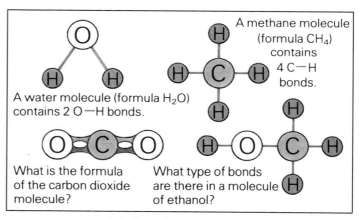

A water molecule (formula H_2O) contains 2 O—H bonds.

A methane molecule (formula CH_4) contains 4 C—H bonds.

What is the formula of the carbon dioxide molecule?

What type of bonds are there in a molecule of ethanol?

The formula of a compound is like an 'ingredients label'. It tells you how many atoms of each element are in the compound.

Forces within a molecule

When molecules are used to make new materials, the atoms have to be broken away from the molecule. So the bonds holding the molecule together have to be broken. Atoms which are difficult to separate have a high **bond strength**. If you know the strength of different bonds in a molecule, you can *predict* the chemical properties of that material.

Look at the data on bond strengths. Which bond is the most likely to break first in the ethanol molecule?

Type of bond

C—O in ethanol

C—H in ethanol

C—H in methane

O—H in ethanol

O—H in water

C—O in carbon dioxide

Relative bond strength

Forces between molecules

Most molecules are very small – even the tiniest amount of a molecular substance contains millions of individual molecules. The bonds (forces of attraction) *within* a molecule are very strong. But the forces of attraction *between* molecules are usually very weak. These weak forces of attraction *between* the many molecules which make up a substance are called **intermolecular forces.** They are very important in determining the **physical properties** of materials. For example, the *greater* the intermolecular forces of a substance, the *higher* its boiling point.

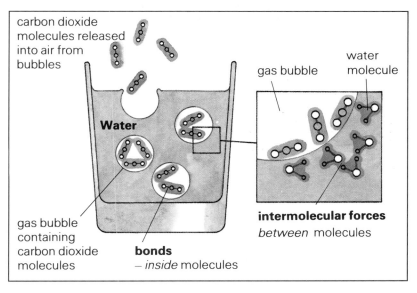

carbon dioxide molecules released into air from bubbles

gas bubble

water molecule

Water

gas bubble containing carbon dioxide molecules

bonds – *inside* molecules

intermolecular forces *between* molecules

This diagram shows the carbonated water used to make fizzy drinks. What does it tell you about the size of the intermolecular forces in a liquid compared with those in a gas? How do you think the intermolecular forces in a solid compare with those in liquids and gases?

There is one carbon atom at the centre of each tetrahedral arrangement of carbon atoms. It is bonded to the four carbon atoms around it.

DIAMOND

tetrahedral arrangement of carbon atoms

Diamond is a macromolecule, containing many carbon atoms joined together by bonds. In order to melt diamond, you would have to break lots of these strong bonds.

Giant molecules

There are some substances that have atoms joined together by bonds but do not consist of individual molecules. They are made up of one very large molecule containing *millions* of atoms joined together by bonds. These giant molecular structures are called **macromolecules.**

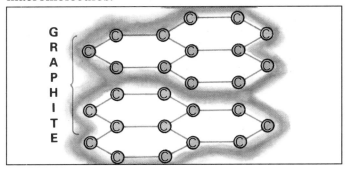

G R A P H I T E

Graphite is another macromolecule made up entirely of carbon atoms. How do the forces in it differ from diamond?

1. A group of molecules called **alkanes** have the general formula C_nH_{2n+2}.
   What is the formula of a molecule of an alkane with:
   a 3 carbon atoms? **b** 10 H atoms?

2. Look at the data on bond strengths. Which two atoms form bonds of different strengths in different molecules?

3. Water and carbon dioxide are produced as hot gases in a car's exhaust. Which one is more likely to react with the iron in the car's exhaust? Give a reason for your answer.

4. Graphite is used as a lubricant because layers of its molecules can slide over each other. Why are they able to slide over each other? Why is diamond *not* used as a lubricant?

3.4 *Covalent bonding between atoms*

Electrostatic forces . . .

Forces make things move – you often see mechanical forces (such as pushes and pulls) making an object move. However there are *other* types of forces such as magnetic forces and **electrostatic forces** (forces between charged particles). Electrostatic forces push or pull, depending on the type of charges involved.

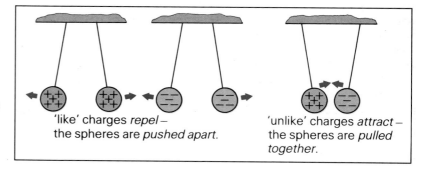

'like' charges *repel* – the spheres are *pushed apart*.

'unlike' charges *attract* – the spheres are *pulled together*.

. . . make chemical bonds

Some atoms of non-metallic elements join together to form molecules. The atoms are held together by strong forces of attraction called **chemical bonds**. These chemical bonds are caused by electrostatic forces. Atoms of elements have no overall charge, but do contain charged particles. **Protons** are *positively charged* particles that are found in the small **nucleus** at the centre of the atoms. **Electrons** are *negatively charged* particles that *move around* the nucleus.

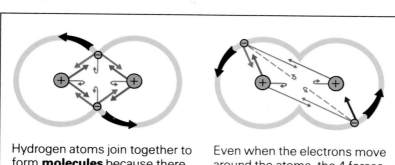

Hydrogen atoms join together to form **molecules** because there are 4 forces of attraction (⇄) but only 2 forces of repulsion (⇄ & ⇄).

Even when the electrons move around the atoms, the 4 forces of attraction are still greater than the 2 forces of repulsion.

The simplest example of atoms joining together to form a molecule is the combination of two hydrogen atoms.

Filling shells

Not all elements have atoms that will join together to form chemical bonds. **Helium**, **neon** and **argon** are a group of atoms that don't form bonds. Chemists call them the **inert gases** – because they are so *unreactive*. In order to explain the inability of some atoms to join with others, chemists proposed that electrons were arranged in **shells** around the nucleus. Each shell has a *limit* to the number of electrons it can hold. Electrons go into the shells in a certain *order*. The **inner shells** (those closest to the nucleus) are always filled *first*. The diagrams show you the number of electrons that can fit into the first three shells.

An atom with *all* its shells full cannot fit any more electrons into these shells. *As a result, it does not form bonds with other atoms.*

Helium atom

Neon atom

Two electrons fill the *first* shell. The **electronic structure** of the shell of helium is: **2**

Eight electrons will fill the *second* shell. The **electronic structure** of neon's shells is: **2, 8**

Eight electrons will also fill the *third* shell.

What is the electronic structure of argon's shells?

Argon atom

Bonding to different atoms

Atoms become more *stable* if they can find a way of filling their outer shells. An atom with an unfilled outer shell of electrons can **share electrons** with another atom which has an unfilled outer shell – this sharing means that both atoms end up with filled shells. The bond formed by the sharing of outer shell electrons is called a **covalent bond**. Fluorine (electronic structure *2,7*) forms one covalent bond when it reacts with a hydrogen atom (electronic structure *1*).

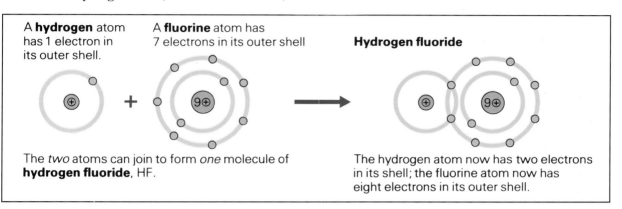

A **hydrogen** atom has 1 electron in its outer shell.

A **fluorine** atom has 7 electrons in its outer shell

Hydrogen fluoride

The *two* atoms can join to form *one* molecule of **hydrogen fluoride**, HF.

The hydrogen atom now has two electrons in its shell; the fluorine atom now has eight electrons in its outer shell.

Not all the outer shell electrons have to be involved in the sharing of electrons. These electrons do not take part in bonding. Oxygen (electronic structure *2,6*) forms *two* covalent bonds with *two* hydrogen atoms.

The nitrogen atom has an electronic structure *2,5*. How many covalent bonds do you think it will form when it reacts with hydrogen atoms? How many hydrogen atoms will become bonded to the one nitrogen atom?

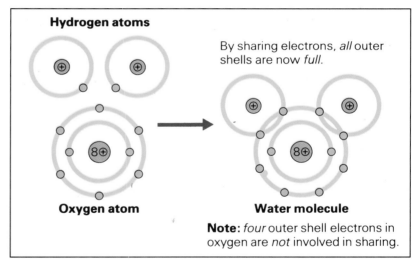

Hydrogen atoms

By sharing electrons, *all* outer shells are now *full*.

Oxygen atom

Water molecule

Note: *four* outer shell electrons in oxygen are *not* involved in sharing.

---

1 What is the electronic structure of the following atoms? (Number in brackets = *total* number of electrons.)
   a boron (*5*); **b** phosphorus (*15*); **c** magnesium (*12*); **d** chlorine (*17*).

2 **a** Which one of the atoms in Q1 has the same number of outer shell electrons as fluorine?
   b Draw the atomic structure of the atom in **a**.
   c How many covalent bonds would you expect this atom to form with hydrogen?

3 The valency of an atom is the number of electrons supplied by the atom for sharing to form a covalent bond. What is the valency of:
   a hydrogen; **b** fluorine; **c** oxygen?

4 Nitrogen (*7*) and phosphorus (*15*) have similar chemical properties.
   a Suggest a reason for this.
   b Name 2 other elements from this spread that you might expect to have similar chemical properties to each other. Why?

5 Draw a diagram to show how electrons are shared to achieve full shells when the following atoms join together to form molecules:
   a A carbon atom (*15*) and 4 hydrogen atoms (*1*);
   b A nitrogen atom (*7*) and 3 fluorine atoms (*9*);
   c How many electrons in each atom are not involved in bonding?

3.5   Polymers

'Setting off' a reaction

'You can't make an omelette without cracking eggs' . . . and you can't make a reaction happen without breaking bonds! Fluorine and oxygen are both elements that take the form of gases made up of molecules. Both elements will react with hydrogen – oxygen reacts so fast with hydrogen that the reaction can cause an explosion. But fluorine reacts even faster with hydrogen – causing an even bigger explosion!

This is because it is *easier* to break a bond in a fluorine molecule than to break a bond in an oxygen molecule. This is why fluorine is a *more reactive* element than oxygen. Chemists use their knowledge of bonds to help *predict* which molecules will react together to form new substances.

Students investigated the reactivity of two closely-related compounds: *ethane* and *ethene*. Both are gases made up of molecules, and both are **hydrocarbons** (molecules containing only the atoms *hydrogen* and *carbon*). The types of bonds in the molecules and their relative strengths are shown here.

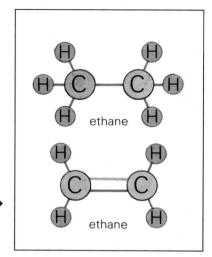

■ Which molecule do you think will be the more reactive?

The students added orange bromine water to test tubes of each gas. If the bromine (in the bromine water) reacts with another molecule, it loses its orange colour. To make the test as fair as possible, they added 30 drops of bromine water to each tube.

	Observations with bromine water
Ethane	Bromine water remained orange
Ethene	The first 12 drops of bromine water went colourless. The remaining drops stayed orange

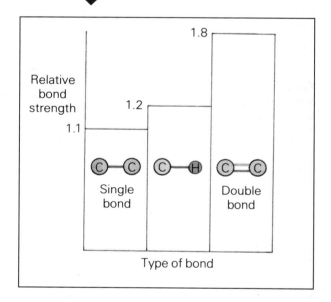

You can see from the results that carbon-carbon double bonds in ethene are more reactive than the carbon-carbon single bond in ethane. But the data on bond strengths shows the double bond to be the stronger of the two, *so you would expect it to be less reactive!*

■ How do you think chemists explain these results?

Which bond will break first in a reaction? If the strongest bond has a relative bond strength of 1, what will be the bond strength of the weak bond?

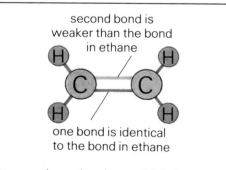

How much weaker do you think the second bond is?
Which one of the two bonds do you think reacts with bromine water?

Making use of reactivity

Reactive molecules containing double bonds can be very useful. Under certain conditions, molecules of this type can be made to join together. Such molecules are called **monomers**. When they react together, monomers form long chains called **polymers**. Plastics, synthetic fibres and fabrics are examples of polymers. Many plastics contain many thousands of carbon atoms which have joined together to form a carbon chain (or backbone). Some plastics have other atoms 'mixed in' as part of their backbone.

Plastics

There are two different types of polymer plastics that can be made, depending on the types of monomers used to make the plastic.

Thermoplastic polymers have *strong* bonds between the atoms in each polymer chain, but *weak* intermolecular forces between the polymer chains. Thermoplastics are flexible and easy to shape by breaking the weak forces between the chains. Heating a thermoplastic causes the polymer chains to break free from these weak intermolecular forces. This means thermoplastics melt quite easily and so have low melting points. ▶

Thermosetting polymers have different properties from thermoplastics. This is because their *structure* and *bonding* give rise to different intermolecular forces.

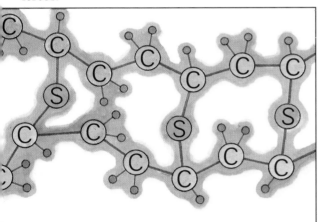

Which bonds have to break before the monomers join together? ▼

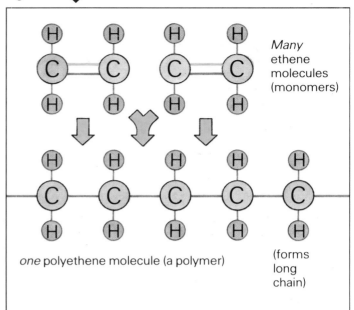

Many ethene molecules (monomers)

one polyethene molecule (a polymer)

(forms long chain)

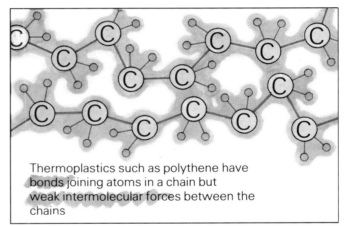

Thermoplastics such as polythene have bonds joining atoms in a chain but weak intermolecular forces between the chains

*This diagram shows **vulcanised rubber** – rubber which contains sulphur atoms between the chains. Thermosetting polymers, such as vulcanised rubber, are much stiffer than thermoplastics. The more sulphur atoms there are between the chains, the stiffer the polymer becomes.*

---

1 | What are the formulas of ethane and ethene?

2 | State two other factors the students (opposite) needed to do to make the tests on the gases fair.

How did they know the C–H bond in ethene does not react?

3 | State two properties of thermosetting polymers that will be different from thermoplastics.

4 | Draw the polymer (with a backbone 6 carbons atoms long) that can be made from 3 monomers like this:

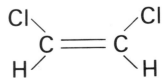

5 | Explain why the vulcanised rubber used in a car tyre needs to contain less sulphur than that used to protect a car battery.

YOU CAN READ MORE ABOUT PLASTICS ON SPREAD 4.6   57

3.6 *Properties and bonding*

'What, no chips?'

This is the age of the 'silicon chip', but silicon has played an important part in our lives long before the 'chip' was invented. About 75% of the earth's crust is made up of **silicates** – materials containing the elements silicon and oxygen. There are over a thousand types of silicates: sand, gemstones (topaz and garnet) and many different clays. The *electronic* properties of the silicon 'chip' are often the focus of attention – but instead this spread looks at how useful silicon compounds are, and how their *structure* and *bonding* determine their *physical* properties and uses.

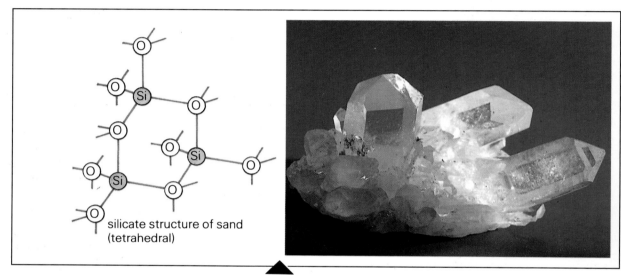

silicate structure of sand
(tetrahedral)

Sand is made up of tiny quartz crystals. The silicon-oxygen bonding makes quartz hard and sand abrasive.

Rigid giant molecules

Sand contains an orderly arrangement of silicon atoms bonded to oxygen atoms to form **silicon dioxide** (silica, SiO_2). The orderly arrangement of atoms leads to a crystalline structure. Pure sand is colourless but iron impurities give it its characteristic yellow or brown colour. Covalent bonds link the atoms into a **giant crystalline molecule** or **macromolecule**. As a result, sand is *hard* and has a *high melting point*. Its hardness has been put to good use in the building trade to make *hardwearing* concrete and mortar.

Slippery layer structures

Silicon and oxygen atoms can join together to form crystalline **hexagonal plates**. An example of this is found in the mineral **mica**. The plates are like sheets of paper lying on top of each other. *Within* each sheet there are covalent bonds, so fairly strong forces hold the atoms in a sheet. The forces of attraction *between* the sheets are *very weak*. As a result, it is easy to split mica into sheets.

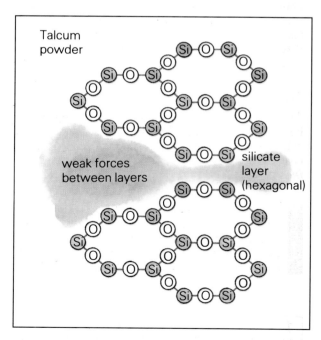

Talcum
powder

weak forces
between layers

silicate
layer
(hexagonal)

*Talcum powder is made of layers of **silicates** – which slide easily over each other.*

58

Ceramics – fired clays

Clays also consist of plates lying on top of each other (as they do in talc or mica). However, when clay is wet, water molecules are able to get in between the layers and it becomes slippery and *easy to shape*. But if the water evaporates *slowly* the clay loses its slippery feel and becomes hard. The process can be reversed by adding water.

In ancient times, once people had learnt how to '*fire*' clay, they were able to build long-lasting homes with **bricks** (rather than stone). They were also able to store food in **pottery** containers -- keeping it fresher for longer. These people had discovered that the properties of clays could be *permanently* changed by heating strongly ('firing'). Water in the clay is driven off by the strong heating and *new bonds* link the layers of silicates together. Clays that have been 'fired' are called **ceramics** and are *very hard*.

Water molecules act as a lubricant in wet clay – like tennis balls trapped between layers of chicken wire! During firing, the chemical change caused by rapid water loss causes new bonds to form in clay – linking silicate layers into a strong giant molecular structure.

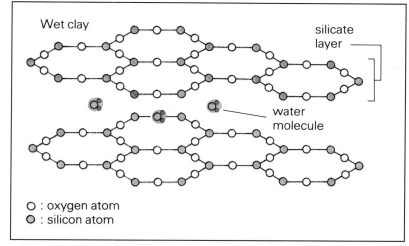

Wet clay — silicate layer — water molecule

○ : oxygen atom
◉ : silicon atom

Fibrous chains

There are silicates which consist of layers rolled into a tube (like rolled-up newspaper). The tubelike structure gives such minerals a fibrous appearance. The most common fibrous minerals are types of **asbestos** – which can be made into sheets (just as wood is made into paper). It was widely used as an insulating material in building – until it was discovered that fibres of a certain size irritate the lungs, and can cause a cancer called **asbestosis**.

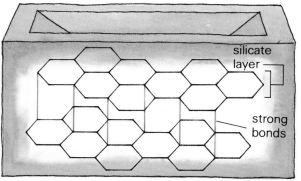

silicate layer — strong bonds

Changing the chain

Chain structures of silicon and oxygen atoms can also be made with different chain lengths. These substances are called silicones. **Silicones** with *short* chain lengths are *liquids*; but as the chain length *increases*, they become *greases* and *rubbery solids*.

Silicone chain

weak forces between molecules

What does this tell you about the forces of attraction between the chains as the chain length increases? Silicones are very useful materials because they *resist most chemicals* and *repel water*. Can you think of any uses for silicones?

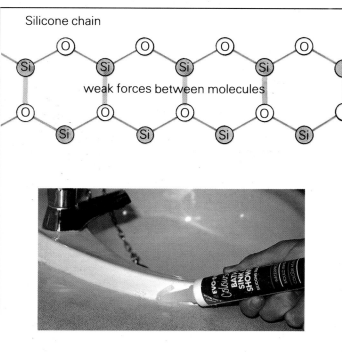

1. Look at spreads 3.3 and 3.5. For each structure here find one similar structure in those spreads. Compare their properties and uses.

3.7 Ionic bonding between atoms

Filling shells . . .

The atoms of metals and non-metals join together in a different way to the covalent bonding between non-metal atoms. *You will need to be familiar with the main ideas about atomic structure to understand how this happens.* (These ideas are explained more fully on Spreads 3.2 and 3.4).

. . . by losing and gaining electrons

Metal atoms have only a few electrons in their outer shells. When metals react with non-metals, the easiest way for metal atoms to obtain a full outer shell of electrons is to *lose electrons*. When metal atoms lose electrons, they are left with more protons than electrons. As a result, the atom is no longer neutral – it is now *positively charged*. A charged atom is called an **ion**. **Metals** *lose electrons to form* **positive ions**.

The electrons lost by the metal atoms are *gained* by the *non-metal* atoms. When a non-metal atom gains electrons, it has more electrons than protons so it becomes *negatively charged*. **Non-metals** *gain electrons to form* **negative ions**.

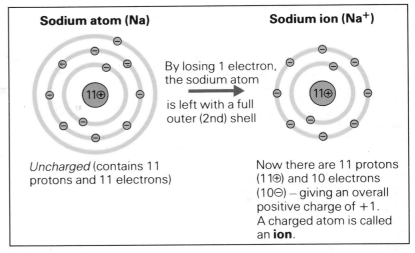

Sodium atom (Na)   **Sodium ion (Na$^+$)**

By losing 1 electron, the sodium atom is left with a full outer (2nd) shell

Uncharged (contains 11 protons and 11 electrons)

Now there are 11 protons (11⊕) and 10 electrons (10⊖) – giving an overall positive charge of +1. A charged atom is called an **ion**.

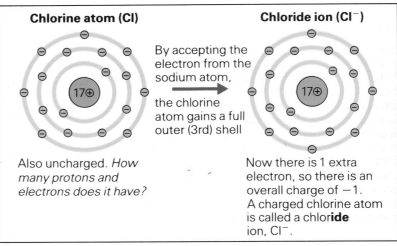

Chlorine atom (Cl)   **Chloride ion (Cl$^-$)**

By accepting the electron from the sodium atom, the chlorine atom gains a full outer (3rd) shell

Also uncharged. *How many protons and electrons does it have?*

Now there is 1 extra electron, so there is an overall charge of −1. A charged chlorine atom is called a chlor**ide** ion, Cl$^-$.

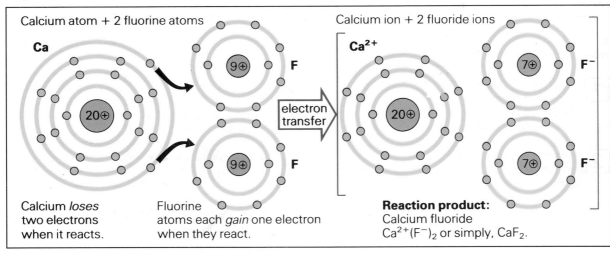

Calcium atom + 2 fluorine atoms   Calcium ion + 2 fluoride ions

electron transfer

Calcium *loses* two electrons when it reacts.

Fluorine atoms each *gain* one electron when they react.

Reaction product: Calcium fluoride Ca^{2+}(F$^-$)$_2$ or simply, CaF$_2$.

The number of electrons lost *by the metal atom is* equal *to the number* gained *by the non-metal atom(s) with which it reacts.*

Charges on the ions

For elements with up to 20 electrons, the number of electrons transferred from the metal to the non-metal depends on the electronic structure.

Different metals with the *same* number of electrons in their outer shells will each normally lose the *same number* of electrons. The size of the positive charge on the metal ion indicates the number of electrons that have been lost.

Similarly, different non-metals with a particular number of electrons in their outer shells will each gain an identical number of electrons. The size of the negative charge will indicate the number of electrons that have been gained.

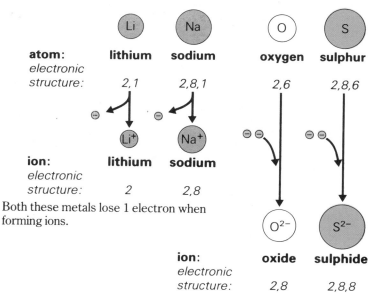

Both these metals lose 1 electron when forming ions.

Both these non-metals gain 2 electrons when forming ions.

Forces of attraction

There is a force of attraction between the oppositely charged ions. This *strong* force acts as a chemical bond, holding the ions together. This type of force between oppositely charged ions is called an **ionic bond**. Unlike most molecules, the ions are not found in small groups but as a **giant structure** in a framework or **lattice**. The greater the charge on the ions, the larger the force of attraction between the ions. A lot of heat energy is needed to overcome these strong forces of attraction – so ionic compounds usually have high melting points. The greater the force of attraction between the ions, the greater the melting points of the **compound** made up of the ions.

Sodium chloride – table salt – is made up of sodium and chloride ions arranged in a lattice.

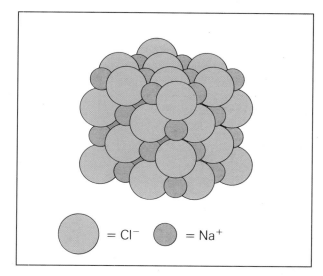

In the following questions, the number in brackets refers to the number of electrons in each atom.

1 By drawing the atomic structures show the transfer of electrons that takes place when Ca(20) reacts with O(8). What is the name and formula of the product?

2 From the following list of symbols of elements; P(15), K(19), N(7), Mg(12), F(9), choose:
  a the atom which forms an ion of charge +2;
  b the atom which forms an ion of charge −1;
  c the atoms which form ions with the same charge.

3 What shape do you think sodium chloride crystals are?

4 Aluminium oxide is made by reacting aluminium(13) with oxygen(8). Their electronic structures are:
Al: 2,8,3; O: 2,6
  a What is the charge on each ion?
  b Aluminium oxide is used to line furnaces. What property makes it an ideal material and why is it better than NaCl?

5 In what ways is ionic bonding similar to covalent bonding?

3.8 *Metallic structures*

Slipping and sliding . . .

Metals consist of **giant structures** containing many millions of atoms. The atoms are packed closely together in **layers**. If you apply a large enough force, the layers are able to *slide* over each other. This is called **slip**. When the layers of atoms slip, the metal takes on a new shape. This helps to explain why, compared to many other materials, metals are easily shaped (**malleable**) and capable of being drawn out into long wires (**ductile**).

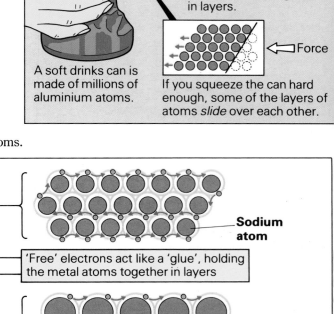

The aluminium atoms are packed closely together in layers.

A soft drinks can is made of millions of aluminium atoms.

Force

If you squeeze the can hard enough, some of the layers of atoms *slide* over each other.

. . . to the breaking point

If the force on the metal is increased, eventually a point is reached when the atoms are *pulled apart* (instead of sliding over each other). When this happens the metal breaks.

The giant structure of metals consists of layers of atoms. In these atoms, some of the outer electrons are *free to move about* from atom to atom. The nucleus of atoms is positively charged and (although the 'free' electrons move around), there is still an **attraction** between the 'free' electrons and the nucleus of each atom. This attraction is called a **metallic bond**. Electrons act like a 'glue', holding the positive ions together.

> Metals which contain the *same* number of 'free' electrons can be grouped together. Look at the models of sodium and potassium. What happens to the strength of the metallic bond if the number of 'free' electrons stays the same, but the size of the atoms increases?

Sodium atom

'Free' electrons act like a 'glue', holding the metal atoms together in layers

Potassium atom

Free electrons	Potassium: *1*	Sodium: *1*
Melting point	Potassium: *63°C*	Sodium: *98°C*
Strength	Potassium is *weaker* than sodium	
Atom size	Potassium is *larger* than sodium	

Other properties

Metals are also very good at transferring heat or electrical energy from place to place. They are said to be **good conductors of heat and electricity**. The transfer of both types of energy is caused by the free moving electrons. The table below shows you the **thermal** (or heat) **conductivity** of different metals; the higher the value, the better the metal is at conducting heat.

> How does this table help to explain why aluminium is a better conductor than sodium?

Thermal conductivity (Wm^{-1}K^{-1})	135	150	220	240
Metal	Sodium	Beryllium	Magnesium	Aluminium
Number of free electrons	1	2	2	3

Stopping the slip

A metal can be made harder and stronger by stopping the layers of atoms from slipping. One way of doing this is to add small amounts of another element. This is called **alloying**. The atoms of the alloying element are different in size to that of the metal and they act as a barrier, stopping the layers of atoms from sliding over each other.

Grain size

Alloying is not the only way of altering the properties of metals. When atoms are arranged in an orderly manner, they form **crystals**. So metals are crystalline. They are made up of many small crystals or grains. The difference in grain size forms patterns on the surface of the metal. You can sometimes see these patterns on thin metal coatings such as the zinc coating on a metal dustbin or bucket. All metal surfaces have similar patterns but they are usually only revealed by the etching action of acids.

The size of the grains has an important influence on the properties of the metal. In general, *the smaller the grain size, the stronger and harder the metal.* Cooling the molten metal very quickly produces a harder stronger metal with smaller grains.

The grain size can also be altered by hammering or rolling. How does this change the properties of a metal?

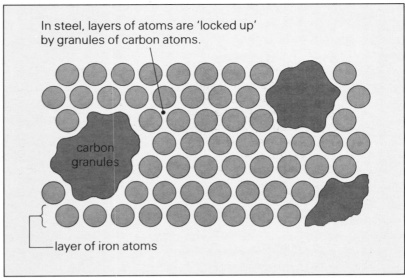

In steel, layers of atoms are 'locked up' by granules of carbon atoms.

carbon granules

layer of iron atoms

*Steel is an **alloy** containing a little carbon mixed with iron.*

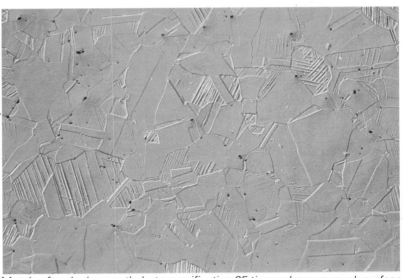

Metals often look smooth, but magnification 25 times shows a rough surface made up of different sizes of grains (crystals).

1. Look at the 'free' electron diagrams opposite. Another metal which can be grouped with sodium and potassium is **lithium** – but it is a *smaller* atom. How will its melting point compare with the other two metals?

2. Explain why:
   a the pattern for electrical conductivities should show the same trend as thermal;
   b potassium is a better conductor than sodium;
   c beryllium is stronger than magnesium.

3. Gold atoms are larger than silver atoms. Which would you expect to be stronger, a gold bracelet or an identical silver bracelet? Why?

4. Draw a model of the alloy bronze made up of 90% copper and 10% tin (a much larger atom). Explain why it is much stronger than pure copper.

5. **Annealing** is a process of cooling metals very slowly. What happens to the grain size when metals are annealed and how will this change their properties?

6. In what ways are metallic, ionic and covalent bonding: a similar; b different?

YOU CAN READ MORE ABOUT METALS ON SPREAD 4.8.

Bursts of energy

Radioactive materials give out radiation all the time. Becquerel detected the energy carried by this radiation using phosphorescent crystals. These gave out light when they absorbed energy from the radiation. At this time, light was thought to be a steady *stream* of energy – and Becquerel wondered if the new radiation was continuous.

One of the **detectors** which revealed the answer is the **spinthariscope**. This contains a screen covered with phosphorescent material. When a radioactive substance is placed near it, the screen glows. Through a magnifying glass, you can see that the glow is made up of many tiny *flashes* of light. From this and other observations, scientists realised that radiation was given out in bursts or *packets* of energy.

Vapour trials

Early experiments showed that the radiation could *ionise* (form charged atoms called **ions**) substances it passed through. Ionisation helps us to 'see' the radiation in a detector called a **cloud chamber**. The cloud chamber is a very cold container full of air saturated with vapour. The vapour will *condense* or form droplets around any ion. When a radioactive substance is placed nearby, radiation passes through the chamber. Each packet of energy forms ions along its path, which can be seen as a vapour trail.

Two kinds of radiation . . .

The pictures below show the trails produced by radiation from a radioactive material. Scientists quickly identified two kinds of trail, which meant two kinds of radiation. These were called α **(alpha) rays** and β **(beta) rays**. The trails were so straight that they were obviously formed by fast-moving **particles**.

What do these pictures tell you about the properties of two types of radiation?

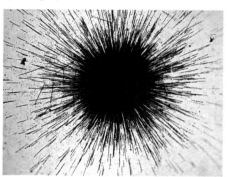
The energy from radium causes dark tracks to form on photographic film.

Vapour trails in a cloud chamber. Here the path of non-colliding α-particles has been coloured green. One α-particle collided with an atom of the cloud, releasing a proton. Their paths have been coloured yellow and red.

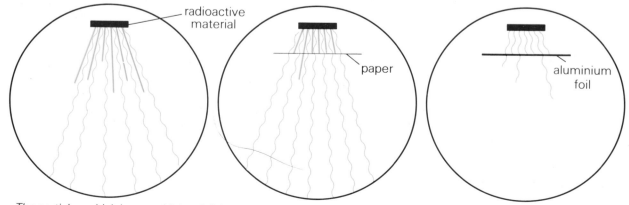

The particles which leave a thicker, brighter trail are called α particles, while the fainter trails are made by β particles.

YOU CAN READ MORE ABOUT IONS ON SPREAD 3.7 AND IN PHYSICS BOOK SPREAD 4.13.

... and a third!

Further investigations revealed *another* kind of radiation. This was not a beam of particles but **electromagnetic radiation**, like light and X-rays. Called γ (**gamma**) **rays**, it was even more penetrating than X-rays and could pass through thick lead sheets.

Some radioactive materials, such as radium, emit all three kinds of radiation – and light and X-rays. Others may emit only one or two kinds.

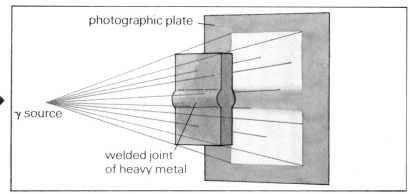

Gamma radiation can even pass through thick metal, especially faults or cracks in welded joints.

photographic plate

γ source

welded joint of heavy metal

A charge on the rays?

Scientists also tried to find out whether any of the radiations carried electrical charges. To do this, they put a cloud chamber in between the poles of a magnet. They knew that if a wire carrying a current (a flowing electrical charge) was put between a magnet, the wire moved. So a beam of charged particles should also be deflected by a magnet – and the *lighter* the particles, the *bigger* the deflection.

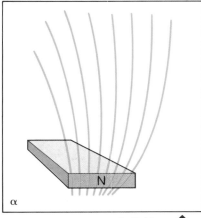

α

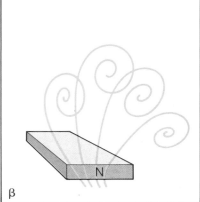

β

α and β rays responded differently to the same strong magnetic field. γ rays were not deflected. What does this tell you about each of the types of radiation?

Probing the atom

The α, β and γ rays seemed to come from the **atoms** of radioactive materials. At this time, an atom was thought to be a sphere containing positively and negatively charged particles *mixed up together*. Scientists wanted to find out more about the atom – and α-particles helped.

When α-particles were fired at metal foil, some of the α-particles bounced back. The α-particles were known to carry *positive* charges and so would be *repelled* by strong positive charges in the foil. But what were these strong positive charges? The scientists Ernest Rutherford suggested that *all* the positive charges in the atom were *concentrated at the centre* forming a positively charged **nucleus**. His ideas led to a new model of the atom – and the discovery of the **proton**.

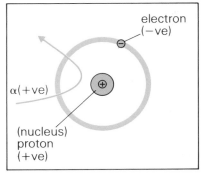

electron (−ve)

α(+ve)

(nucleus) proton (+ve)

A model of the atom. It was later discovered that the nucleus of most atoms contains neutrons (which have no charge) as well as protons.

---

[1] Why did scientists think that radiation was a continuous stream of energy?

[2] What evidence showed that the radiation was made up of 'bursts' of energy?

[3] a How did the cloud chamber help scientists to identify two kinds of radiation?
   b What were they?
   c How do the properties of the two kinds of radiation differ?

[4] a Which kinds of radiation were deflected by a magnetic field? What does this tell you?
   b Which kind of radiation was deflected *most*? What does this tell you?

[5] What safety precautions would you use when handling radioactive materials? (Think about the properties of α, β and γ rays.)

YOU CAN READ MORE ABOUT ATOMS AND ATOMIC STRUCTURES ON SPREADS 3.2 AND 3.4.

3.10 Patterns in radioactivity

Patterns among the elements

The new model of the atom helped in *classifying* the elements. Chemists had already arranged elements in order in the **Periodic Table**. They did this using the *properties* of the elements and the *relative masses* of atoms of the elements – but these did not always agree! The order of the elements was found to follow perfectly the *number of protons* in the atom.

A modern Periodic Table shows the symbol of each element *and:*

- its **atomic number** – the number of protons in the nucleus
- its **mass number** – the number of protons and neutrons in the nucleus.

Sections of the Periodic Table in which elements are arranged in order of their atomic number.

| | | | | | | 1 H 1 hydrogen | 4 He 2 helium |
| 11 B 5 boron | 12 C 6 carbon | 14 N 7 nitrogen | 16 O 8 oxygen | 19 F 9 fluorine | 20 Ne 10 neon |

| 133 Cs 56 caesium | 137 Ba 56 barium | 139 La 57 lanthanum |
| 223 Fr 87 francium | 226 Ra 88 radium | 227 Ac 89 actinium |

| 207 Pb 82 lead | 209 Bi 83 bismuth | 210 Po 84 polonium | 210 At 85 astatine | 222 Rn 86 radon |

| 232 Th 90 thorium | 231 Pa 91 protactinium | 238 U 92 uranium |

238 —— mass number

U —— chemical symbol

92 —— atomic number

Uranium

→ Radium

→ Radon

→

Part of the radioactive series of uranium decay, which eventually finishes with stable lead. ▲

Modern alchemy

Ancient scientists called alchemists dreamed of changing or **transmuting** elements – particularly cheap metals – into gold. At the beginning of this century, scientists knew that atoms of an element could not change *during a chemical reaction*. Then Rutherford and other scientists studied the elements in radioactive materials carefully – and came to a startling conclusion: *radioactive elements transmute as they give out radiation!*

This is because radioactivity is *not* a chemical change. It involves the *nucleus* of an atom and is a **nuclear reaction**. When the nucleus of an atom emits α or β particles, the atom **decays** into the atom of a *different* element. The atom may decay again and again forming a series of elements known as a **radioactive series**.

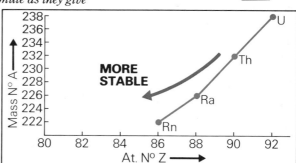

This graph shows how the mass number and atomic number change as uranium decays to radon. At each stage, an α particle is emitted. Can you work out what an α particle is? ▲

Patterns of decay

By studying many radioactive series, and noting the positions in the Periodic Table of the elements formed, scientists found patterns of decay. For example, look at the positions in the Periodic Table of the elements formed in the section of the uranium series shown. What pattern can you see?

Nuclear reactions

The nucleus of an atom contains protons and neutrons held together by strong **nuclear forces**. Many nuclei are *stable* and don't undergo nuclear reactions easily. But some nuclei, particularly very large ones, are *unstable*. They can break down or decay, ejecting energy and particles.

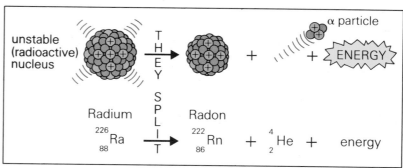

A radium nucleus emits an α particle and energy as it decays.

YOU CAN READ MORE ABOUT THE PERIODIC TABLE SPREADS 2.1–2.7.

Isotopes

Close study of atoms and nuclei led to another revelation – all the atoms of an element are *not* necessarily the same. Atoms of the same element may take different forms, called **isotopes**. The isotopes of an element have the same number of protons but *different numbers of neutrons*. For example, the most common isotope of carbon ($_6^{12}$C) has six protons and *six* neutrons. Another isotope of carbon ($_6^{14}$C) has six protons and *eight* neutrons.

All the atoms of an isotope have the same mass number. So isotopes are often referred to by their mass number. The two isotopes of carbon may be written **carbon 12** (or C-12) and **carbon 14** (or C-14).

Radioisotopes

An isotope with unstable nuclei is radioactive and is called a **radioisotope**. An element may have some stable and some unstable isotopes. Most carbon (99 per cent) is made up of stable isitopes, mainly carbon 12. Carbon also has a number of radioisotopes, including carbon 14. The lighter elements tend to have mainly stable isotopes, while the isotopes of the heaviest elements are usually radioisotopes.

The rate of decay

A radioisotope decays all the time, and as each atom decays it emits a burst of radiation. You can find out about the decay by detecting and counting each burst. This reveals that the decay of atoms is *random* – any atom may decay *at any time*. Ten atoms may decay one second and none the next. So how can you find the *rate of* decay?

The answer is to count the bursts over a long enough period of time and to repeat the count at intervals. If you plot a graph of your findings, a pattern emerges – a **decay curve**. As atoms decay, there are fewer left to decay. So the rate of decay slows down, forming a curve.

Another pattern is that the length of time for a particular radioisotope to lose *half* of its radioactivity is *constant*. This time is called the **half life** of the radioisotope. Very unstable isotopes may have half lives of less than a second. The more stable radioisotopes can have half lives of thousands of years.

Key
- ◦⁻ electron
- ⬤ neutron
- ⊕ proton

The simplest atom

$_1^1$H **hydrogen**

$_1^2$H **deuterium** (isotope of hydrogen)

$_1^3$H **tritium** (isotope of hydrogen)

New element $_2^4$He **helium**

The simplest element, hydrogen, has three isitopes. Heavier elements may have far more.

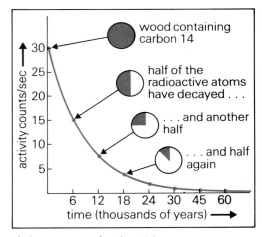

A decay curve of carbon 14.

- wood containing carbon 14
- half of the radioactive atoms have decayed . . .
- . . . and another half
- . . . and half again

1. How did the new model of the atom help chemists work out the order of the elements?

2. a What is an α-particle?
   b Radon decays emitting an α-particle. What element does radon change into as it decays?
   c This element also decays emitting an α-particle. What new element is formed?

3. An ore of uranium was found to contain impurities that did not come from the surrounding rocks and minerals.
   a How do you think the impurities came to be there?
   b What do you think the impurities might be?

4. An element used to be defined as 'a pure substance containing only one kind of atom'.
   a Why is this definition wrong?
   b Write a more accurate definition.

5. The carbon 14 in the wooden handle of an axe found in Egypt decayed at the rate of 13 counts per minute. When new, the handle would have given a count of about 20 a minute. Estimate how old the handle is. (Carbon 14 has a half life of 6000 years.)

3.11 Radiation and health

Long-lasting radioactivity

Nuclear fission, whether in a nuclear reactor or an atom bomb, produces radioactive daughters. Each of these will decay – and may decay to another radioisotope, forming a radioactive series. So fission results in a huge mixture of radioisotopes.

This table shows some of the radioisotopes produced by fission. Each emits one or more of the radiations α, β and γ – and these can damage living organisms. As you can see from their half lives, some will emit radiation for a very long time.

Homing in on the body

Both α and β radiations seldom travel more than 1 metre and are stopped by paper or foil. Like light, γ radiation spreads out and loses its intensity the further away you are. So radioactive materials are safe if you stay away from them. The trouble is – you can't!

Many elements are absorbed by your body. Iodine is used in your thyroid gland. Strontium is used to make bones. Other elements are used in chemical processes in your cells. Just as carbon 14 is taken in along with stable carbon, your body may absorb radioisotopes of any element it needs.

Isotope	Half life	Radiation emitted	Used by body
thorium $^{234}_{90}$ Th	24 days	α	–
thorium $^{230}_{90}$ Th	80 000 yrs	α	–
radon $^{220}_{86}$ Rn	52 sec.	α	no but can be breathed in
plutonium $^{239}_{94}$ Po	24 400 yrs	α	no but can be breathed in
iodine $^{131}_{53}$ I	8.07 days	$\beta\gamma$	yes into thryroid gland
strontium $^{90}_{38}$ Sr	28.1 yrs	$\beta\gamma$	yes into bones

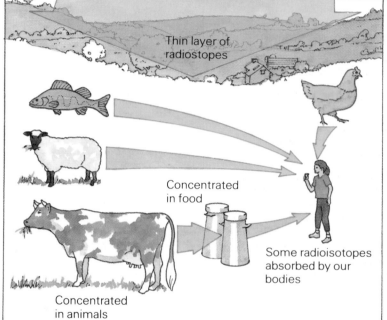

Thin layer of radiostopes

Concentrated in food

Some radioisotopes absorbed by our bodies

Concentrated in animals

Radiation can become concentrated by passing through our food chain and then into our food.

Damaging cells

Radiation can damage the atoms used to make living cells. This damage can usually be repaired by your body, if it does not involve massive numbers of cells. But if the **genes** in cells are damaged, the cells can change or *mutate*, and some may become cancerous.

The different kinds of radiation vary in the extent or **quality (Q)** of the damage they cause. The α-radiation is thought to be the most damaging and has a Q value of 20. It is a stream of relatively large particles – helium nuclei – that collide with atoms and molecules, stripping electrons away to produce ions. The much smaller β particles and γ radiation are much less likely to collide with atoms and so are thought to be less dangerous. They both have a Q value of 1.

These irregular chromosome shapes show how the 'genetic message' of a cell can be altered by radiation. The cell may then develop into a different, possibly cancerous, cell.

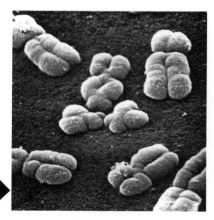

YOU CAN READ MORE ABOUT GENES AND GENETIC DAMAGE IN BIOLOGY BOOK, SPREAD 4.15.

Measuring the damage

The more radiation we receive, the greater the risk of damage, so it is important that we keep a check on it. The amount of radiation – the number of radioactive decays per second – is measured in **becquerels (Bq)**. One Bq is equal to 1 radioactive decay per second.

But how much damage will the radiation cause? To find this out, we need to work out the amount of radiation *energy* absorbed by our bodies. This depends on the *quality*, Q, of the radiation and the amount of energy (J) received by a kilogram (kg) of flesh (measured in **greys, Gr**). This gives the **radiation dose** measured in **sieverts (Sv)**:

$$1\,\text{Sv} = 1\,\text{Gr} \times Q$$

In one year the average person should *not* receive more than about 0.005 Sv.

situation	dose (Sv)	effects
treatment of	100	cells *destroyed*
tumour/cancer	10	
accident/war	1	cells damaged
	.1	(short term)
maximum allowed	.01	possibility of
in industry		cancer
		(long term)
natural radiation (1 yr)	.001	
chest X-ray	.0001	
holiday in area of	.00001	possibility of
granite rock	.000001	genetic change (affecting future generations)

Even very low doses of radiation may cause genetic change, which can appear after many generations.

Are you getting your sieverts?

Radiation is all around you – and not just from nuclear reactors and atom bombs. Radioactive materials have been present in the Earth since its formation. Cosmic radiation continually bombards the atmosphere forming more radioisotopes.

All these radioactive sources produce **background radiation**. You are subjected to background radiation all the time. The amount of radiation you actually receive will depend on, for example, where you live, your occupation, your lifestyle and what you eat.

1 'The problem with the atom bomb isn't the blast'. Do you agree? Give reasons for your answer.

2 Draw a pie chart to show the amounts of background radiation we receive from different sources.

3 An accident at a distant nuclear power plant has released radioisotopes into the environment. Using the information on the opposite page, write an article for a local newspaper, explaining how the accident could affect people in *your* area.

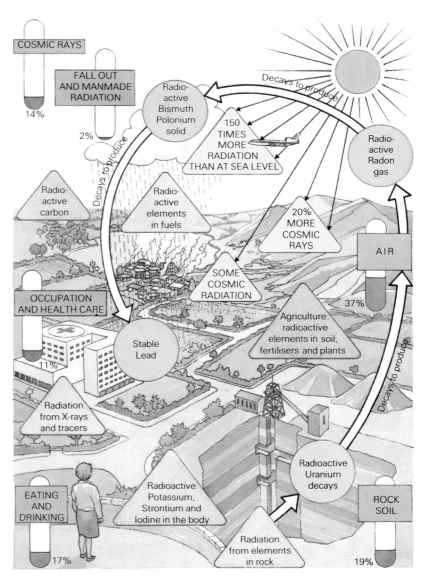

4.1 *Getting the right recipe*

Making cakes

If you want to make a cake, having a list of the ingredients in a recipe book isn't enough. You also need to know the *relative* amounts of each ingredient – what proportions of margarine, flour, eggs etc. you need. If you know these, you can make the cake any size by altering the *amounts* of the ingredients but keeping their *relative* amounts the same. For example if you need 150 g margarine and 200 g of flour to make a smallish cake, you'll need 225 g of margarine and 300 g of flour to make a larger one.

You make a cake by using the correct materials and the right ingredients in the right amounts. A chemist makes metals, plastics, glass and many other useful materials in the same way.

Making materials

When you make a material such as a metal alloy, a new plastic or glass you will also need the list of ingredients. This is contained in the word equation. But although this tells you the ingredients to use, or **reagents** as they are called, it doesn't tell you how much you need nor the amount of products that will be formed.

This word equation tells you the ingredients used and formed when copper oxide and carbon are mixed together then heated.
Copper oxide + carbon → copper + carbon dioxide.
But it doesn't tell you the amount of carbon and copper oxide to use nor how much copper and carbon dioxide will be formed. ▼

The right amount

You can find the relative amounts of each reagent from the equation containing the chemical formulae – the **balanced symbol** equation – for the reaction. This gives you information about the *type* and *number* of atoms of the elements in the reaction. You can also find the relative atomic mass (RAM) of each element from the Periodic Table (*see 2.1 and 2.3*). The relative mass of each compound in the equation is the *sum* of the RAMs of its elements. Once you have calculated the *relative* mass of all the reagents and products you can work out how much of each element or compound to use (assuming you can fix the mass of the substance) since their relative masses will always stay the same. The table shows the relative masses of the products and reagents needed when copper oxide is reduced by carbon to form copper and carbon dioxide is given off. How much carbon do you need to reduce 40 g of copper oxide and how much copper will be formed?

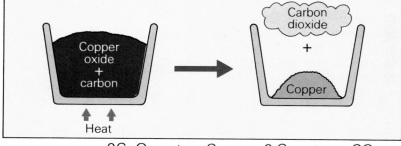

	2CuO		C	2 Cu	CO₂	
Type of element	Cu	O	C	Cu	C	O
Number of atoms of each element	2	2	1	2	1	2
RAM of each element	64	16	12	64	12	16
Relative mass of compound	2 × 64 + 2 × 16 = 160		1 × 12 = 12	2 × 64 = 128	1 × 12 + 2 × 16 = 44	

From the relative masses of the compounds, 160 g of copper oxide are reduced by 12 g of carbon to form 128 g of copper and 44 g of carbon dioxide or 80 g of copper oxide are reduced by 6 g of carbon to form 64 g of copper and 22 g of carbon dioxide. Note that in each case the relative amounts of reagents and products are the same and the mass of reagents = mass of products.

Making plastics

Plastics are large molecules called polymers made by joining together smaller molecules called monomers. Different plastics can be made by joining together different types of monomers. The plastic polytetrafluoroethene (PTFE) is made by joining together tetrafluororethene monomers. Look at the relative mass of the molecules in the equation.

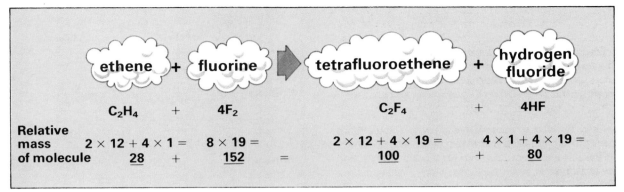

ethene	+	fluorine	→	tetrafluoroethene	+	hydrogen fluoride
C_2H_4	+	$4F_2$		C_2F_4	+	$4HF$

| Relative mass of molecule | $2 \times 12 + 4 \times 1 =$ __28__ | + | $8 \times 19 =$ __152__ | = | $2 \times 12 + 4 \times 19 =$ __100__ | + | $4 \times 1 + 4 \times 19 =$ __80__ |

> How much ethene and fluorine would a chemical factory need to use to produce 25 tonnes of tetrafluoroethene?

Making glass

Ordinary glass is a mixture of materials. It is made by heating together silicon oxide, sodium carbonate and calcium carbonate.

> How much sand would a glass company need to use to react with 5.03 tonnes of sodium carbonate and 5 tonnes of calcium carbonate?

Look at the Periodic Table on 2.1 to find the RAMs of the elements in the questions.

Glass is a product of sand, limestone and sodium carbonate.

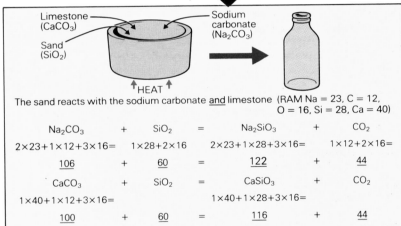

The sand reacts with the sodium carbonate and limestone (RAM Na = 23, C = 12, O = 16, Si = 28, Ca = 40)

Na_2CO_3	+	SiO_2	=	Na_2SiO_3	+	CO_2
$2 \times 23 + 1 \times 12 + 3 \times 16 =$ __106__	+	$1 \times 28 + 2 \times 16$ __60__	=	$2 \times 23 + 1 \times 28 + 3 \times 16 =$ __122__	+	$1 \times 12 + 2 \times 16 =$ __44__
$CaCO_3$	+	SiO_2	=	$CaSiO_3$	+	CO_2
$1 \times 40 + 1 \times 12 + 3 \times 16 =$ __100__	+	$1 \times 28 + 2 \times 16$ __60__	=	$1 \times 40 + 1 \times 28 + 3 \times 16 =$ __116__	+	__44__

1 Iron is made in a blast furnace by the reduction of iron oxide, using carbon monoxide.

$$Fe_2O_3 + 3CO \rightarrow 2Fe + 3CO_2$$

How much iron oxide needs to be reduced to obtain 28 tonnes of iron?

2 How much ethanol (C_2H_6O) could be made from the fermentation of 0.5 kg of grape sugar?

$$C_6H_{12}O_6 \rightarrow 2C_2H_6O + 2CO_2$$

3 A limestone company heats limestone ($CaCO_3$) to produce lime (CaO). How much limestone does it need to heat each day to make 112 tonnes of lime?

$$CaCO_3 \rightarrow CaO + CO_2$$

4 The reaction between chlorine and ethene is used to make chloroethene (vinyl chloride), the monomer used to make PVC. How much chloroethene could be made from 142 kg of chlorine?

$$C_2H_4 + Cl_2 \rightarrow C_2H_3Cl + HCl$$

5 Baking powder, sodium hydrogencarbonate ($NaHCO_3$), decomposes on heating to produce carbon dioxide (CO_2) which makes cakes rise.

$$2NaHCO_3 \rightarrow Na_2CO_3 + H_2O + CO_2$$

a What mass of carbon dioxide is produced by heating 8.4 g of baking powder?
b If the volume of 44 g of CO_2 is 24 litres at room temperature and pressure, what will be the volume of the CO_2 in **a** at the same temperature and pressure?

YOU CAN READ MORE ABOUT PLASTICS ON SPREAD 4.6.

Chemical changes

Getting a reaction

In the Middle Ages, alchemists tried to obtain gold from cheap metals, but failed. The reason for this was simple – since gold wasn't contained in one of the starting materials (reactants), they couldn't get gold as one of the products!

Hydrogen and oxygen are simple chemicals. When hydrogen gas burns in oxygen gas, water is formed because the oxygen and hydrogen **react** together. The simplest way of representing this **chemical reaction** is to use a *word equation* as shown here.

Hydrogen and oxygen both exist as pairs of **atoms** *bonded together* as **molecules**. Water is made up of molecules containing *two* hydrogen atoms bonded to a *single* oxygen atom. You can represent the reaction by drawing the molecules taking part. You can see that starting with 1 molecule of oxygen (O_2), you will form 2 molecules of water (H_2O) when the oxygen combines with 2 molecules of hydrogen (H_2). Although this is a very clear way of describing a reaction, it is rather longwinded.

Balanced equations

Another representation uses **chemical symbols** to show what happens in reactions. When you do this the equation is called a *symbol equation*. This gives the *same* information as drawing the molecules, but in a much shorter form.

In *all* reactions, the type and number of atoms present is the same *before* and *after* the reaction. This means a chemical (symbol) equation includes the same type and number of atoms on each side – and the equation is said to '**balance**'.

	Reactants	Products
Word equation	Hydrogen + Oxygen	Water
Draw molecules		
Symbol equation	$2H_2 + O_2$	$2H_2O$
Check: Do atoms balance?	$4H + 2O$	$4H + 2O$

Look at the 'Check' step. There are 4(H) atoms and 2(O) atoms on both sides, so the equation is balanced.

There are two more examples of chemical equations below. Can you balance them? ▼

	Reactants	Products
Word equation	Ethanol + ___?___	Carbon Dioxide + ___?___
Draw molecules		
Symbol equation	$C_2H_6O + \underline{3}$ ___?___	___?___ ___?___ $+ 3H_2O$
Check: Do atoms balance?	$2C + 6H +$ ___?___ ___?___	___?___ ___?___ $+ 6H + 7O$

	Reactants	Products
Word equation	Nitrogen + ___?___	Ammonia
Draw molecules		
Symbol equation	$N_2 + \underline{?}$ ___?___	2 ___
Check: Do atoms balance?	$2N +$ ___?___ ___?___	___?___ ___?___ $+ 6H$

Releasing energy . . .

As well as making new materials, most chemical reactions release energy. You eat food to provide you with energy. The energy from food keeps you warm and allows you to do everything from just breathing to running. The energy is released by a chemical reaction called **respiration**.

. . . by breaking and making bonds

In a chemical reaction the atoms are rearranged by making new **bonds**. Energy is first *used* to *break* the bonds in some of the molecules. This forms 'free' atoms that are then able to join together (in a different arrangement) to make new molecules.

Energy is *released* to form new bonds when the 'free' atoms join together. Some of this energy is used to break the bonds in *other* molecules – providing the energy for the reaction to continue. The overall energy change arising from the reaction is the *difference* between *the energy needed* (for bond breaking) and the *energy released* (by bond making). An energy profile can be drawn for any chemical reaction, showing this difference in energy. This difference is called the **enthalpy change** of the reaction and is given the symbol ΔH.

When fuels are burnt in oxygen, they release a lot of energy. Most common fuels consist of **hydrocarbon** molecules (containing only atoms of hydrogen and carbon). The table shows you the amount of energy released by burning $1\,m^3$ of different fuels (all gaseous hydrocarbons). This amount of energy is called the **calorific value** of the fuel.

In batteries, chemicals release electrical energy which can be changed into light or sound or movement or . . .

*An energy profile for the combustion of methane. When methane burns in oxygen, E_{OUT} is greater than E_{IN}, so $E_{IN} - E_{OUT}$ is negative. When ΔH is negative, the reaction is **exo**thermic and **releases energy** as heat (and light).*

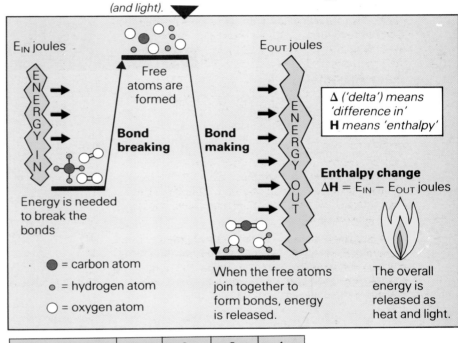

Δ ('delta') means 'difference in'
H means 'enthalpy'

Enthalpy change
$\Delta H = E_{IN} - E_{OUT}$ joules

Energy is needed to break the bonds

- ● = carbon atom
- ◦ = hydrogen atom
- ○ = oxygen atom

When the free atoms join together to form bonds, energy is released.

The overall energy is released as heat and light.

Carbon atoms in 1 molecule of fuel	1	2	3	4
Calorific value **MJ**/m^3	38.5	67.5	96.5	125.5

1 Balance the following equation:
$$C_3H_8 + O_2 \rightarrow CO_2 + H_2O$$

2 Give one example of an energy change involving: **a** heat; **b** light; **c** electrical energy.

3 Write an equation for the combustion of methane shown in the energy profile above.

4 Draw an energy profile for an **endothermic** reaction where ΔH is **positive**.

5 The EEC has suggested the U.K. replace the **B**ritish **T**hermal **U**nit for measuring the energy of gas. What would you replace it with?

6 Look at the table above showing calorific values. What would be the calorific value of a fuel with 6 carbon atoms?

7 The Gas Board charges about £15 for 38.5 MJ of energy. If they supplied you with $20\,m^3$ of methane (CH_4), what would your gas bill be?

4.3   Rates of reaction

Same reaction, different rates

Some chemical reactions such as those in a firework are very fast and spectacular yet others, for example the rusting of iron, are much slower. The *rate of reaction* is a measure of how fast the reaction can take place. The pictures show what happens when acids react with limestone and marble chips (both different forms of calcium carbonate). Does the reaction always occur at the same rate? What factors might alter the rate of reaction?

Acid rain can eat away at limestone figures over years but . . . .

. . . . the reaction between marble chips and acid in the laboratory can be over in a couple of minutes.

Measuring rates

You can investigate the factors that change the rate of reaction between calcium carbonate and an acid in the laboratory. If the acid used is hydrochloric, then the products of the reaction are calcium carbonate, water and carbon dioxide:

$$CaCO_3 + 2HCl \rightarrow CaCl_2 + H_2O + CO_2$$

In order to find out the rate of reaction, you need to *measure* something in the reaction that changes with *time*. One of the things you could measure is the mass of material in the flask. This is decreasing all the time because carbon dioxide is escaping into the air during the reaction. Alternatively you could collect the carbon dioxide and record the amount of gas collected every minute using an apparatus like this.

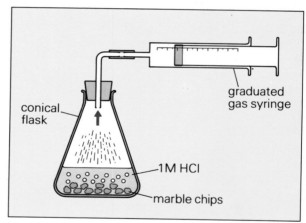

You can measure the volume of CO_2 collected at regular intervals using a gas syringe like this.

Effect of increasing concentration

A group of students decided to investigate the effect of increasing the acid concentration on the rate of its reaction with calcium carbonate. They did the experiment twice, first using 1M acid and then 2M acid which is twice as concentrated. In order to make the test fair, they used the same mass of marble chips and the chips were all about the same size in both cases. What else did they need to do in order to make the test fair?

They compared the results of both experiments by recording their results on a graph. The steeper the slope of the graph, the faster the rate of the reaction. What does the graph of their results show you about the effect of the concentration of the acid on the rate of the reaction as it proceeds?

How much faster is the reaction using 2M HCl compared to 1M HCl? ▶

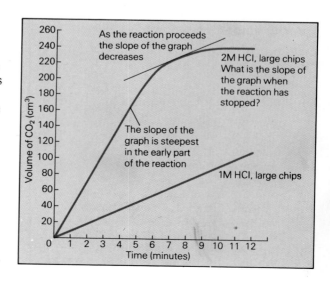

Effect of changing particle size

Another group of students decided to investigate the effect of changing the size of the marble chips. The conditions they used are shown in this picture. Their teacher looked at the experiment and noticed some errors. Can you see what they were?

After correcting these errors, the students recorded two sets of results using large chips and then small chips with 1M acid in each case. Their results are shown in the table. What do they show you about the effect of *decreasing* the particle size on the rate of reaction?

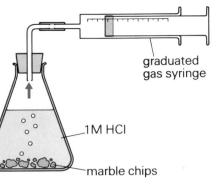

graduated gas syringe

1M HCl

marble chips

Time (mins)	Volume of CO_2 (cm^3)	
	① 1M HCl Large chips	② 1M HCl Smaller chips
2	18	54
4	36	108
6	54	162
8	72	206
10	90	230
12	108	240

Explaining reaction rates

For a chemical reaction to take place the particles of each element must collide. Not all collisions between particles will lead to a chemical reaction since some will not have enough energy. For reactions carried out at the same temperature, if you can increase the chance of a collision then a reaction is more likely – the rate of reaction will be greater.

By increasing the concentration of ○ particles, there is a greater chance of collisions with the ○ particles. ▼

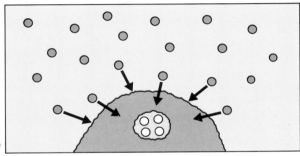

By breaking the larger solid into smaller pieces, you can increase its surface area so there is more chance of ○ colliding with the ○ particles. ▼

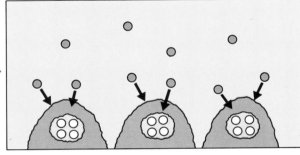

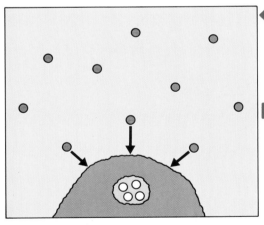

Only those ○ particles on the surface of the large solid can collide with ○ particles.

Can you see why increasing the concentration of the acid (increasing the number of particles) or breaking up the marble chips into smaller pieces will increase the rate of reaction?

1. Look at the pictures at the beginning of the spread. Suggest two reasons why the laboratory reaction is faster.

2. What other method(s) could the students have used to measure the volume of carbon dioxide?

3. Describe how you would measure the rate of reaction between acid and marble chips by following the change of mass of the chips with time. What precaution would you have to take to ensure the accuracy of your results?

4. Plot a graph of the results in the table above. Use the graph to predict when the first experiment will be complete. Draw on the graph the shape of the curve you would predict for
   a twice the mass of the smaller chips
   b half the mass of powdered marble.

5. How could a group of students modify the experiment to investigate the effect of temperature on the rate of reaction?

6. Flour dust can react explosively with air. Why isn't this a problem with wheat grain?

4.4 *Food deterioration*

Rotten food

When you buy pre-packed food you'll notice it has a sell-by date. The fresh fruit you buy – fruit, meat veg – will 'go off' after a certain time. All food becomes unsuitable to eat and harmful to health after a certain time. Food deterioration can be caused by microscopic living organisms – **micro-organisms**, such as bacteria. Micro-organisms need food for energy and for growth (increasing their numbers). There are many different types of micro-organisms which thrive on different types of food.

Sour milk

Just as *you* need sugar for energy, so bacteria rely on sugars for their energy. Milk contains milk sugar, **lactose**, which bacteria feed on. The milk sugar is broken down or **hydrolysed** by water molecules and this process provides energy for the bacteria. Certain molecules in the bacteria speed up this process – these are called **biological catalysts** or **enzymes**.

The conversion of lactose in milk to lactic acid depends on the number of bacteria present.

Lactic acid is produced as a waste product of this process and this affects the flavour and the texture of the milk – it makes it taste and look sour. As more lactic acid is produced in the milk, its pH decreases.

▌Look at the graph. Why does the reaction slow down after about 40 hours? ▶

The overall process can be represented by the equation:

lactose + water → lactic acid

Sour grapes

Not all micro-organisms are harmful to food. The ancient Egyptians, for example, were already brewing alcohol from yeast which feeds on fruit and other plants. Yeast belongs to the class of micro-organisms called fungi and feeds on carbohydrates in plants. Enzymes in the yeast break down the carbohydrates into ethanol (an alcohol) and carbon dioxide. This releases energy. The overall process (called **fermentation**) can be represented by the equation:

carbohydrate → ethanol + carbon dioxide
$$C_6H_{12}O_6 \rightarrow 2C_2H_6O + 2CO_2$$

▌You can measure the rate of the reaction by counting the number of bubbles of carbon dioxide produced in a minute. This graph shows that the reaction rate depends on the temperature. What is the best temperature range for getting yeast to make ethanol and carbon dioxide fastest when ▶ brewing beer?

The mould growing on this yoghurt belongs to a group of micro-organisms called fungi.

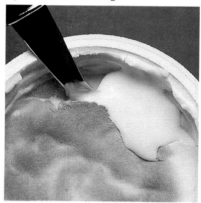

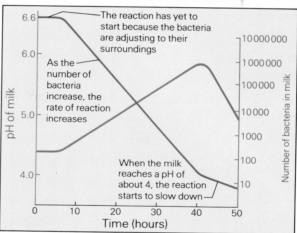

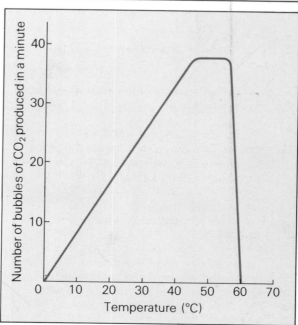

Browned off

Some foods, for example many fruits and vegetables, contain enzymes in their cells. Apples contain an enzyme which speeds up the formation of a brown polymer (a large chain molecule). If the cells are ruptured or broken, this enzyme is exposed and it reacts with the air. This causes the apples to go brown – you've probably seen this many times.

Some students carried out an investigation into the effects of pH and temperature on apple browning. Look at their results. What pH does the enzyme work best in? ▶

Effect of temperature and catalyst on reaction rate

Molecules at the same temperature don't all have the same energy. Some molecules are moving faster than others. This means their energies are spread over a wide range at a certain temperature. The graph shows you the distribution of energies you would expect to find in a large number of molecules at two different temperatures. As you can see the distribution changes with temperature. For a chemical reaction to take place, the molecules must have a certain minimum energy (E on the graph). Only those molecules with an energy greater than this minimum energy will take part in a chemical reaction. From the graph you can see that more molecules will react at T_2 than T_1. But *without* an increase in temperature, more molecules will still react if a catalyst – or enzyme – is added. A catalyst provides an alternative lower energy pathway for a chemical reaction.

How does the graph help to explain why the rate of a chemical reaction is faster for a catalysed than for an uncatalysed reaction *at the same temperature?*

1. Explain how food preservation is helped by
   a freezing   **b** pickling in vinegar
   c cooking then sealing in cans.

2. Draw a graph to predict the growth of yeast cells at different temperatures.

3. A group of students investigating fermentation using yeast noticed that at every temperature the number of bubbles of carbon dioxide was uneven at first then became steady. Explain what was happening.

4. **a** Why do you need to handle apples carefully?
   b Look at the picture of the apple browning experiment. Why haven't the apples turned brown at 0°C and 100°C?

5. State two reasons why lemon juice is often added to fruit cocktails.

Contents of each tube (cm³)					
	A	B	C	D	E
Water	5	–	–	5	5
Acid	–	5	–	–	–
Alkali	–	–	5	–	–
Apple juice	3	3	3	3	3

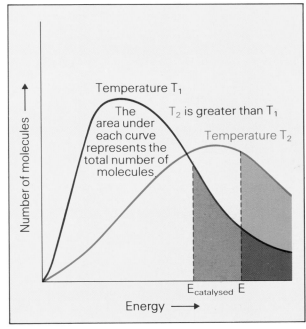

The minimum energy for an uncatalysed reaction is 'E' on the graph. At temperature T_1, ▬▬ molecules react but at the higher temperature, T_2, ▬▬ and ▬▬ molecules react since more molecules have energies greater than the minimum energy needed. The rate of reaction increases at the higher temperature because more molecules are reacting. If a catalyst is added the rate of reaction increases without the need for a higher temperature.

6. Look at the graph above. What area would you shade to show how many more molecules react in the catalysed reaction at temperature T_2?

YOU CAN READ MORE ABOUT POLYMERS ON SPREAD 3.5.

4.5 *Flammable materials*

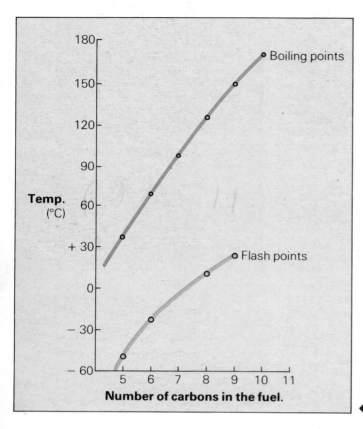

In November 1987, 31 people died in a horrendous 'flash point' type fire at Kings Cross London Underground station. It is important for all of us to know about how different materials burn and what actually happens when they burn – fire is a very serious business.

Starting to burn

When most fuels catch fire it is the vapours from the fuel that are burning not the solid or liquid part. A petrol fire occurs in the petrol vapour, just above the surface of the liquid, not in the liquid itself. When a material is heated directly by a spark or flames the vapours will only ignite if their temperature is above a certain value. The minimum temperature above which a vapour will ignite is known as the **flash point** of the material. The harder it is to vapourise a material, the higher will be its flash point.

When vapours are compressed, for example by pistons in a diesel engine, they become hot. The more they are compressed, the hotter they become. At a certain temperature a vapour will ignite even though there is no direct source of heat. This temperature is known as the **self ignition temperature** of the material.

◀ *What does this graph show you about the flash point of a material as its boiling point increases?*

Burning up . . .

To burn a material you need oxygen, which is present in the air, and a source of heat. Materials such as petrol or natural gas which burn very easily have low flash points and are said to be highly **flammable**. Materials that don't burn are said to be **non-flammable**. Limestone, for example, is non-flammable – it breaks down into simpler substances when it is heated.

During burning, oxygen adds onto the elements of which the material is made, producing **oxides** and energy is released as heat and light. This is why there is often a flame – a mixture of heat and light – released by the burning fuel. Petrol, which is a mixture of compounds containing the elements hydrogen and carbon, burns to form water (hydrogen oxide) and carbon dioxide. The addition of oxygen to a substance is called **oxidation** and the chemical name for burning is **combustion**.

Incomplete burning

When some materials burn they often produce harmful substances because the burning has been incomplete. This incomplete burning is caused by lack of sufficient oxygen – in other words complete oxidation cannot take place. Petrol, for example, will also produce carbon monoxide (CO) and smoke or unburnt carbon (C) as well as water and carbon dioxide. Compounds which contain nitrogen as well as carbon and hydrogen such as polyurethane also produce hydrogen cyanide (HCN).

Materials need heat and oxygen before they burn.

A burning cigarette may be all that is needed to start a serious fire.

Materials which produce lots of smoke on burning contain high proportions of carbon to hydrogen. Benzene contains 6 carbons for every 6 hydrogens (C_6H_6). Methane contains 1 carbon for every 4 hydrogens (CH_4). The greater proportion of carbon to hydrogen in benzene compared with methane means that it burns with a much smokier flame than methane.

A lot of carbon in the form of soot, or smoke is produced which can make breathing very difficult.

Some furniture still contains soft padding made of polyurethane which means poisonous invisible gases such as hydrogen cyanide and carbon monoxide are produced.

Domestic fires in the home are quite common and can be very dangerous, often because of the toxic gases given off during the burning of certain materials.

Stopping the burn

To put out a fire, you need to remove the oxygen, heat or fuel. Cooling the fire by water removes the source of heat and takes the temperature of the vapours below their flash point.

Smothering a fire by using foams, powder – even a blanket, cuts off the supply of oxygen. This stops the chemical reactions occurring in the flames. However, since smothering does not cool the fuel, the temperature of the vapours could still rise above the flash point and **reignition** may occur.

Small fires may be put out using fire extinguishers. The type of extinguisher used depends on the nature and location of the fire.

Look at the table which shows 5 different types of extinguisher. Why do you think Class C fires (flammable gases) are put out by smothering-type extinguishers and not by cooling?

Type	Extinguishes mainly by	Class A fires (paper, wood, textile)	Class B fires Flammable liquids	Class C fires Flammable gases
Water	Cooling and smothering	✓	✗	✗
Foam	Smothering and cooling	✓	✓	✗
Carbon dioxide	Smothering	✗	✓	✓
Dry powder	Smothering	✓	✓	✓
Halon	Smothering	✓	✓	✓

1 Why is it dangerous to smoke near petrol but not near cooking oil?

2 Why do diesel engines not need spark plugs to ignite the fuel?

3 Look at the graph.
   a Which fuels will ignite at about room temperature (20°C)?
   b What is the boiling point and flash point of the fuel with 7 carbons?
   c What is the flash point of the fuel with 10 carbons?

4 What do you think would be formed when propane (C_3H_8) is burnt **a** completely **b** incompletely?

5 Which fuel will burn with the smokier flame, propane (C_3H_8) or toluene (C_7H_8)?

6 a What do you think are the most likely causes of death in domestic fires?
   b What do you think are the most likely cause of these fires?

7 Look at the table.
   a Which extinguishers can only be used for class A fires?
   b Which extinguisher do you think gives the least risk of the fuel reigniting?
   c Which types of extinguisher would you *not* use if your chip pan full of very hot oil caught fire? What could you do if you did not have a suitable extinguisher to hand?

4.6 *From oil to plastics*

Too much or too little

The distillation of crude oil provides us with many useful products but we use these products in differing quantities. Some fractions are in great demand but are in short supply. Heavier fractions, such as fuel oil and bitumen, make up the larger proportion of some crude oils but they are not needed as much as lighter fractions such as petrol.

Fraction	Amount present in crude oil (%)	Current every day demand (%)
Liquified petroleum gas	2	4
Petrol	16	24
Naphtha	10	4
Paraffin	15	7
Diesel oil	19	23
Lubricating oil Fuel oil Bitumen	48	38

What does this table tell you about some of the production problems oil refineries are faced with?

Small molecules from large molecules

The heavier fractions that are produced in surplus quantities are made of long chain hydrocarbons. Hydrocarbon molecules are made of hydrogen and carbon atoms joined together in a chain. The backbone of this chain consists of carbon atoms (*see 3.5*). If these long chains could be broken up into smaller sections it would provide a way of getting rid of the excess of heavier fractions and of making more of the lighter fractions.

Heating the long molecules of fuel oil and bitumen causes them to vibrate more. Continued heating will vibrate the molecules enough to break the carbon chain so that long chain molecules can be shortened. The breaking of the chain is called **cracking**. Cracking can also be induced by chemical methods, known as catalytic cracking.

*Heating a hydrocarbon molecule strongly causes its carbon chain to break producing smaller molecules. This is called **cracking**.*

Cracked but useful

Cracking is a very important process because it turns the less useful fractions of crude oil like fuel oil into more widely needed fractions with smaller molecules such as petrol and paraffin. When a hydrocarbon molecule is cracked, the number of hydrogen and carbon atoms remains the same but they have been rearranged. One part of the chain contains carbon atoms all of which are surrounded by four other atoms. No more atoms can be attached and it is said to be **saturated**. Petrol and paraffin are examples of saturated molecules.

The other part of the carbon chain, produced by cracking, contains some carbon atoms surrounded by only three atoms. More atoms can still be attached to these and the molecule is said to be **unsaturated**. These unsaturated molecules are useful products from cracking. An example of an unsaturated molecule is ethene.

Butane is a saturated hydrocarbon. No more atoms can be attached

Ethene is an unsaturated hydrocarbon. More atoms can still be attached

*Cracking produces a **saturated** and **unsaturated** hydrocarbon.*

Making giant molecules . . .

Ethene molecules can react together to form long chains containing many thousands of carbon atoms. The process of joining small molecules together to form a long chain molecule is called **polymerisation**. The chain molecule that is formed is called a **polymer** and the small molecules that are used to make it are called **monomers**. 'Poly' means 'many' so the long molecular chain that is formed of ethene units is '*poly*ethene' or *poly*thene for short. Different polymers can be made from other unsaturated molecules like styrene – *poly*styrene.

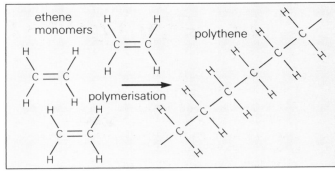

*Ethene monomers can be joined together to form polythene. This is called **polymerisation**.*

. . . to put to good use

Polythene, polystyrene, nylon are all **plastics**. We use the term plastic because of the properties of these long chain molecular materials. Plastic is really only another word for polymer. As you will notice if you look around you, today we really do live in a plastic world. . .

Different forms of plastic have different properties. Each of the properties give rise to different uses.

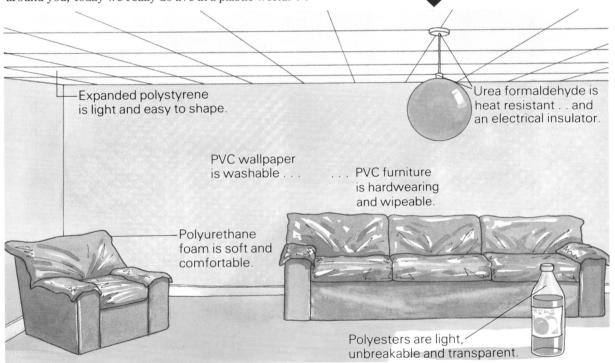

Expanded polystyrene is light and easy to shape.

Urea formaldehyde is heat resistant . . and an electrical insulator.

PVC wallpaper is washable . . .

. . . PVC furniture is hardwearing and wipeable.

Polyurethane foam is soft and comfortable.

Polyesters are light, unbreakable and transparent.

---

1 Look at the table at the top of the opposite page.
  a Which fractions from crude oil show a greater demand than their supply?
  b Which fraction shows the greatest shortfall between its supply and demand?
  c Why would the demand for each product change, depending on the time of year?

2 **a** Draw another diagram to show two different products of the cracking of the hydrocarbon.
  b Draw the shape of the polymer made from the unsaturated monomer unit which you have just drawn in part **a** above.

3 **a** Draw the shape of a saturated hydrocarbon containing 6 carbon atoms.
  b Draw the shape of an unsaturated hydrocarbon containing 3 carbon atoms.

4 By using catalysts, the cracking process can be made to happen much faster and at a lower temperature. Why is this so important in industry?

5 What properties of a plastic do you think make it an ideal material for a **a** watering can **b** hosepipe **c** plant pot?

6 Why do some people think the use of crude oil as a fuel is wasteful of resources?

A growing problem

Every living organism needs food – the animals and plants that you eat also need food. To produce the large amounts of food needed by humans today, farmers need to make sure that their crops grow well and stay healthy. Plants need essential elements, some of which they take from the soil through their root system. These elements must be put back into the soil or the plants will not continue to grow properly. Nature can do this – but not quickly enough to satisfy the increasing human demand for food. Farmers try to solve the problem by adding artificial fertilisers.

Without the use of fertilisers, you would not have as much food to choose from . . . can you think of any disadvantages to using fertilisers?

Nitrogen – an essential element

Nitrogen is one of the elements that plants need to survive. It is a very common element – it makes up almost four-fifths of the air you breathe! So why do farmers buy nitrogen fertilisers? Why can't all plants take it directly from the air?

Nitrogen, like oxygen and fluorine, exists in nature as nitrogen molecules, N_2. These N_2 molecules are remarkably unreactive. Nitrogen (like phosphorus, the other non-metallic element in the same group) doesn't react with water. It also has a very low solubility in water. This means most plants can't absorb it on its own through their roots. It has to be changed into compounds which are water soluble for plants to take it in.

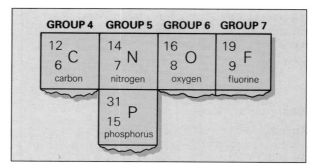

Nitrogen is a non-metallic element. How many electrons does it have in its outer shell and what is its valency?

Soluble compounds of nitrogen

Although nitrogen is a very unreactive gas, it can react with other elements. In nature, the large amount of energy released by lightning helps nitrogen and oxygen in the air to react and form nitrogen monoxide.

$$N_2 + O_2 \rightarrow 2NO$$

The nitrogen monoxide quickly reacts with more oxygen to form nitrogen dioxide.

$$2NO + O_2 \rightarrow 2NO_2$$

Nitrogen dioxide is an oxide of a non-metal and, like other non-metal oxides, it dissolves in water to form an acidic solution. When mixed with air and water, it forms nitric acid.

$$4NO_2 + 2H_2O + O_2 \rightarrow 4HNO_3$$

Like phosphorus, nitrogen also forms a hydride called ammonia, NH_3. It is a colourless gas with a pungent smell and is used in smelling salts . . .

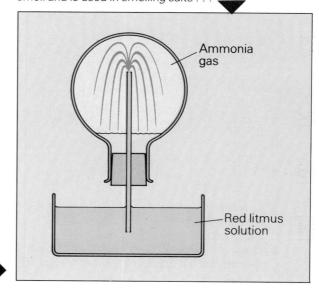

Ammonia gas

Red litmus solution

This flask contains ammonia gas. A small amount of water from the middle tube dissolves all the ammonia and a fountain is produced. What does this show you about the solubility of ammonia in water and the pH of the resulting solution?

The Haber process

Ammonia and nitric acid are soluble nitrogen compounds but neither are suitable for adding directly to the soil as fertilisers. Can you suggest why?

Chemists knew how to change both these into compounds which were less soluble in water, had a pH nearer to 7 and could be more easily put on the soil – the problem was how to make them in large quantities. In 1911, Haber, a German chemist, discovered that ammonia could be made directly from nitrogen and hydrogen. Both reagents are available in large quantities – nitrogen from the air and hydrogen from the reaction between water and natural gas. The elements are converted into ammonia using an iron catalyst and suitable conditions of temperature and pressure.

$$N_2 + 3H_2 \rightarrow 2NH_3$$

The gaseous mixture at the end of the reaction contains about 18% ammonia. This is removed by cooling and the unused nitrogen and hydrogen are recycled.

If ammonia is mixed with air and passed over a heated catalyst (platinum/rhodium alloy) at 1000° C it is **oxidised** into nitrogen monoxide which can be converted to nitric acid:

$$4NH_3 + 5O_2 \rightarrow 4NO + 6H_2O$$

Making nitrogen fertiliser

Ammonia is an alkali or soluble base, so a solution of ammonia in water will react with acid to form a salt. Ammonia solution reacts with nitric acid to form ammonium nitrate – a white solid salt.

$$NH_3 + HNO_3 \rightarrow NH_4NO_3$$

Ammonium nitrate is soluble in water but not as soluble as ammonia, its pH is nearer to 7 than either ammonia or nitric acid and it can be made into granules that are easily added to the soil.

1. Fertilisers can drain into rivers and streams causing pollution. Do you think that only organic farming, which uses manure as a fertiliser, should be allowed?

2. Draw the structure of the ammonia molecule, showing how nitrogen and hydrogen share electrons to achieve full shells.

3. Limestone, calcium carbonate $CaCO_3$, is often added to acidic soil. Write an equation to show how it neutralises nitric acid.

4. Look at the graph showing the different yields of ammonia in the Haber process. If the pressure used was 200 atm., what was the temperature of the reaction and why do you think it was chosen?

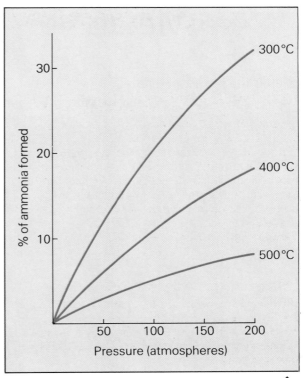

The yield of ammonia depends on the pressure and temperature chosen. Why do you think the reaction is not carried out at room temperature?

Ammonium nitrate is a very common nitrogen fertiliser.

5. How does the use of a catalyst help to speed up the production of ammonia?

6. A company produces 1020 tonnes of ammonia every day. How much nitric acid does it have to produce to react with this ammonia and how much fertiliser will it make?

YOU CAN READ ABOUT THE NATURAL CYCLE OF NITROGEN IN BIOLOGY BOOK, SPREAD 2.7.

4.8 *Metals*

Metals are useful materials . . .

Metals have characteristic properties that make them useful.

Steel, a mixture of iron and carbon, is **malleable**. It can be easily shaped.

Metals like aluminium are **ductile**. They can be drawn out into wires or cables.

Metals such as aluminium or copper are good conductors of heat.

Silver globules of mercury can be obtained from red mercuric oxide by heating.

Zinc   Silver   Magnesium

This diagram shows what happens when three different metals are placed in acid. What does it show you about the reactivity of magnesium compared to the other two metals?

. . . . locked into ores

Some metals, such as gold, are found as "free" metals – that is pure metals – not chemically combined to other elements. Metals such as gold do not combine easily with other elements. However, most metals are found in the Earth chemically combined with other elements in the form of a compound called a **metal ore.** The metal then has to be **extracted** from the ore. Oxygen and sulphur are two elements that are often present in ores, tightly combined with the metal. For example, iron and oxygen combine together to form the ore, haematite, which has the chemical name iron oxide. This compound has completely different properties to the original elements iron and oxygen.

There are three ways of separating metals from the other elements present in ores – using heat, chemical or electrical energy.

The reactivity of metals

Some metals are more **reactive** than others. This means they can be chemically changed very easily. In order to separate a metal from its ore chemically, use is made of differences in reactivity. Some metals react with acids, releasing bubbles of hydrogen gas. The more reactive the metal, the more hydrogen is produced.

The league table of reactivity

By looking at other reactions involving metals, the metals can be placed in a league table of reactivity called the **reactivity series**. The higher a metal's position in the league table, the more reactive it is. Look at the table. It can help you to predict the reactivity of different metals with acids.

Using chemical energy-competition reactions

If two metals compete for the same element, the more reactive element *always* "wins" the competition. Thus the reactivity series can be used to dislodge a wanted metal from its ore, by using a more reactive metal. For example if aluminium and iron oxide (haematite) are heated together, molten iron and aluminium oxide are produced. The aluminium is higher in the reactivity series and so is more reactive than the iron. The aluminium will compete with the iron for the oxygen and will "grab" the oxygen from the iron to give pure iron and aluminium oxide. This is called a **competition reaction**.

Using electrical energy

Sometimes it is not possible to supply enough chemical and heat energy to obtain metals from their ores. This is particularly true when trying to obtain metals at the top of the reactivity series from their ores. Aluminium could not be obtained from its ore by a competition reaction with zinc since zinc is less reactive than aluminium. In such cases electrical energy can provide all the energy that is needed. The electricity is passed through the hot molten ore. The energy provided by the electricity is sufficient to separate the metal from its ore.

Non metal elements can also be used in competition reactions. Coke is a form of carbon and when heated to high temperatures in a blast furnace the carbon (in the hot coke) will remove oxygen from the iron oxide producing molten iron.

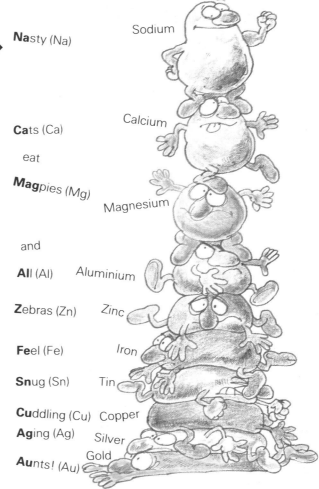

Nasty (Na) — Sodium
Cats (Ca) — Calcium
eat
Magpies (Mg) — Magnesium
and
All (Al) — Aluminium
Zebras (Zn) — Zinc
Feel (Fe) — Iron
Snug (Sn) — Tin
Cuddling (Cu) — Copper
Aging (Ag) — Silver
Aunts! (Au) — Gold

Maybe this will help you remember the reactivity series!

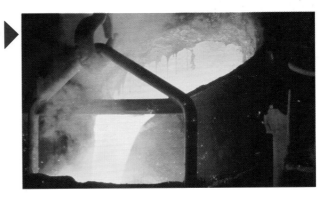

1 State two properties of metals and one example of how each property is used.

2 Why is gold found as a "free" metal and not combined with oxygen?

3 Look at the diagram on the opposite page.
   a Place the three metals in order of reactivity, starting with the most reactive first.
   b Predict which metals would react with acids more vigorously than magnesium.
   c Suggest a metal that you think will not react with acids.
   d If you had to test your answer to **b** and **c** what conditions are needed to make sure the test would be fair?

4 a Where would you place carbon in the reactivity series?
   b Why can't carbon be used to obtain aluminium from aluminium oxide?
   c Name a metal that could be used to obtain aluminium from aluminium oxide in a competition reaction.
   d Name an alternative method of obtaining aluminium from aluminium oxide.

4.9 Corrosion of metals

Corroding away

Metals are very important materials but under certain conditions they can be changed to compounds with less useful properties. When this occurs the metals are said to **corrode** and have to be replaced or discarded. Rusting is the particular name given to the corrosion of iron.

Some corroded metals are also dull. They lose their attractive appearance. ▼

When a metal such as copper corrodes it is no longer as good a conductor of electricity. ▼

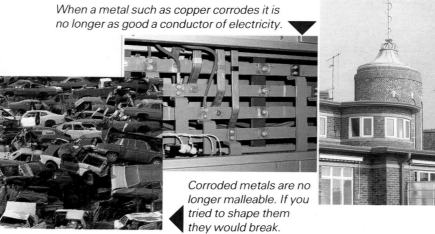

▲ *When metals such as iron rust or corrode they lose their strength.*

Corroded metals are no longer malleable. If you tried to shape them they would break. ◀

Conditions for rusting

A group of students decided to investigate what conditions are needed for rusting. They put some iron nails into test tubes containing different substances and then left them for a few days. These diagrams show the results the students obtained. What did they decide was always needed for rusting to occur?

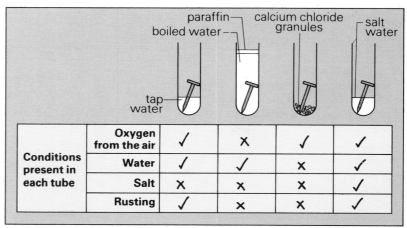

tap water — paraffin — boiled water — calcium chloride granules — salt water

Conditions present in each tube	Oxygen from the air	✓	✗	✓	✓
	Water	✓	✓	✗	✓
	Salt	✗	✗	✗	✓
	Rusting	✓	✗	✗	✓

These diagrams show the results the students obtained. What do you think they decided was always needed for rusting to occur?

Stopping the rust

One way to prevent iron from rusting is to seal its surface. This protects the iron from chemical attack by the oxygen and water which cause rusting. However, once the seal is broken the unprotected iron will rust. This causes the surface to blister, exposing fresh iron so the rusting continues.

Oil lubricates the chain but also protects it.

Paint protects the frame.

Chrome protects the chain wheel and parts of the wheels and handlebar.

Rusting can be prevented in a number of different ways.

What a sacrifice!

A more effective way of preventing iron rusting is to use **sacrificial protection**. A metal which is more reactive than iron, such as zinc, is painted onto the surface of the iron. (*See reactivity series, 2.8 and 4.8*). Because zinc is higher in the reactivity series it reacts first and corrodes instead of the iron. It "sacrifices" itself for the iron. If the surface is scratched or only partly covered, the zinc still provides protection from rusting because the water and oxygen will react with the zinc first, even if there is iron around.

The same group of students carried out another series of experiments to test the process of sacrificial protection. These diagrams show the results they obtained after leaving the samples in plain water for a few days.

Zinc is bolted onto a ships hull. It rusts instead of iron because it is more reactive.

What do these results tell you about the reactivity of tin compared to iron?

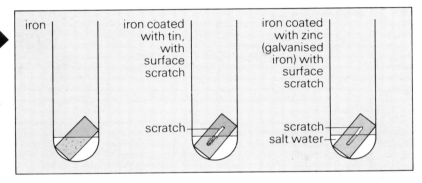

Self protection

Some metals, like aluminium, protect themselves by forming a protective oxide layer which blocks further corrosion.

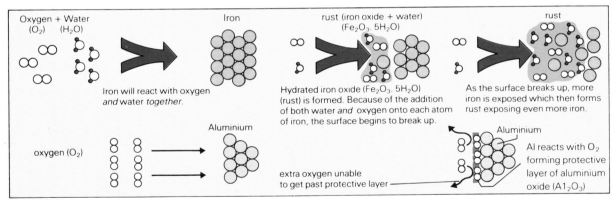

1. Why does rusting cost the country millions of pounds every year?

2. In the first of the students' investigations:
   a. what do you think is the purpose of
      i. the calcium chloride granules
      ii. the paraffin
   b. why was the water boiled?
   c. what effect did salt water appear to have on rusting?

3. If chromium only provides protection from rust until it is scratched, what does this tell you about its reactivity compared to iron?

4. Name another metal that could have been bolted onto the ship's hull instead of zinc. Give a reason for your answer.

5. In the second of the students' investigations:
   a. what did the group need to do to make sure the test is fair?
   b. what do the results tell you about the reactivity of zinc compared to iron?
   c. what would have happened if the iron had been coated in copper instead of zinc?

6. Why don't aluminium window frames corrode?

4.10 The blast furnace

Iron is used in many industries ranging from transport to building homes and even furniture. It is very strong and can last many years. To use iron, it first has to be extracted from its source – the Earth.

Digging deep

You may have seen rocks being used for building materials or for making roads. Some rocks also contain minerals which are a valuable source of metal compounds called **ores**. Haematite or iron ore, for example, is a compound of iron. Rock containing iron ore can be obtained from the ground by either opencast or underground mining. The amount of iron ore in the rock may vary from as little as 20% to as much as 70%. After mining, the ores are crushed to a fine powder then screened or sieved to remove some of the worthless material. The concentrated iron ore is then made into pellets in a special plant before being shipped to a blast furnace.

Iron ore used for making iron is dug out of the ground.

Releasing the metal . . .

Metals, including iron, are chemically combined with other elements in the rock to form a compound called a metal ore. Oxygen is one of the elements often present in the ores, chemically combined to the metal. When oxygen combines with another element it forms an oxide. Iron ore contains iron and oxygen combined together as **iron oxide**. In order to obtain iron from iron oxide, the oxygen has to be removed. The removal of oxygen from a substance is called **reduction**.

There are different types of iron oxide but haematite is iron(III) oxide, Fe_2O_3.

. . . by using a reducing agent

A substance that removes oxygen from another substance is called a **reducing agent**. The reducing agent in the reduction of iron oxide to iron is carbon monoxide. This is formed at the very high temperatures found in a blast furnace. Coke – a purer form of the element carbon than coal – combines with oxygen from a blast of hot air to form carbon monoxide, CO.

$$2C + O_2 \rightarrow 2CO$$

The carbon monoxide then reduces the iron oxide in the ore to iron. At the high temperatures inside the furnace the iron formed is molten.

$$Fe_2O_3 + 3CO \rightarrow 2Fe + 3CO_2$$

The coke not only acts as a raw material for the reducing agent carbon monoxide, but its reaction with the oxygen from the air supplies much of the energy needed to keep the furnace very hot.

The reaction between coke and air is **exothermic** – it releases heat to the surroundings.

Cleaning up the mess

The main impurity in iron ore is sand or silicon dioxide, SiO_2. This has such a high melting point that it would not melt in the blast furnace and would form an ash that would be very difficult to remove. To overcome this difficulty, the ore is mixed with limestone, $CaCO_3$. At the high temperatures inside the furnace the limestone is thermally decomposed into calcium oxide, CaO, and carbon dioxide, CO_2.

$$CaCO_3 = CaO + CO_2$$

The calcium oxide reacts with the sand to form calcium silicate, $CaSiO_3$, or slag. The slag has a much lower melting point than the sand and, like the iron, becomes molten.

$$CaO + SiO_2 = CaSiO_3$$

The molten iron and molten slag sink to the bottom of the furnace. The slag floats on top of the iron and both can be tapped off separately. The iron produced by the blast furnace is about 95% pure. It is called **pig iron**.

Molten iron is tapped off from the blast furnace at regular intervals.

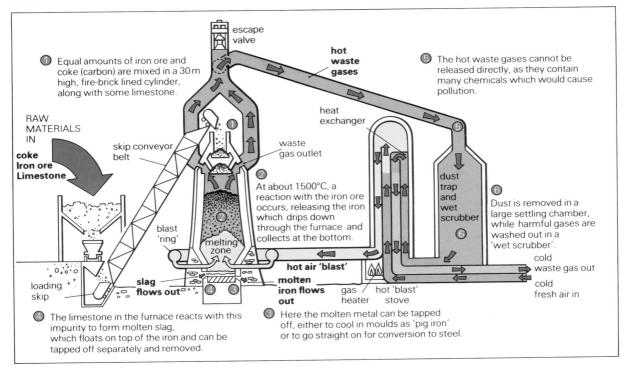

1. Equal amounts of iron ore and coke (carbon) are mixed in a 30 m high, fire-brick lined cylinder, along with some limestone.

2. At about 1500°C, a reaction with the iron ore occurs, releasing the iron which drips down through the furnace and collects at the bottom.

3. Here the molten metal can be tapped off, either to cool in moulds as 'pig iron' or to go straight on for conversion to steel.

4. The limestone in the furnace reacts with this impurity to form molten slag, which floats on top of the iron and can be tapped off separately and removed.

5. The hot waste gases cannot be released directly, as they contain many chemicals which would cause pollution.

6. Dust is removed in a large settling chamber, while harmful gases are washed out in a 'wet scrubber'.

escape valve, hot waste gases, heat exchanger, waste gas outlet, RAW MATERIALS IN coke Iron ore Limestone, skip conveyor belt, blast 'ring', melting zone, loading skip, slag flows out, hot air 'blast', molten iron flows out, gas heater, hot 'blast' stove, dust trap and wet scrubber, cold waste gas out, cold fresh air in

---

1. Name four raw materials used in the blast furnace.

2. Why is the furnace called a **blast** furnace?

3. Coke has two separate functions in the production of iron. What are they?

4. Oxidation is the addition of oxygen to a substance. Give an example from the spread of a substance that has been oxidised.

5. Look at the diagram of the furnace. How does the heat exchanger help to make great energy savings?

6. Why do you think blast furnaces work continuously all the year round?

7. Draw a flow diagram for the production of iron. Start with the raw materials and show how by a series of stages they help to convert iron ore into iron.

4.11 Sulphuric acid

A very useful chemical

Sulphuric acid, H_2SO_4, is an acid commonly used in school laboratories. The acid is also found in cars as battery acid. Its use, however, is not confined to car batteries and school laboratories. More sulphuric acid is made worldwide than any other chemical. Over 100 million tonnes of sulphuric acid is made each year. This is because the acid is an essential chemical for many industrial processes. These processes range from making fertilisers to manufacturing paints and plastics.

Product	Amount of H_2SO_4 used worldwide (millions of tonnes)
Fertilisers	30
Paints	14
Detergents	10
Artificial fibres	8
Plastics	4

Sulphuric acid is used in the production of many basic items.

Raw materials

Sulphuric acid is made from an oxide of sulphur called sulphur dioxide, SO_2. This is a gas and is made from sulphur and oxygen. Some parts of the world, such as Texas and Poland, have large deposits of sulphur. Air is a useful source of oxygen since it is a mixture of gases which contains 20% oxygen. Sulphur burns in air (or oxygen). The oxygen combines with the sulphur to form sulphur dioxide.

$$S + O_2 \rightarrow SO_2$$

The addition of oxygen to a substance is called **oxidation**.

Large tankers unloaded molten sulphur, by pipeline, to sulphuric acid plants.

The Contact process

Almost all the sulphuric acid is made by the **Contact process**. The raw material, sulphur dioxide, is mixed with air. This mixture is fed into a converter containing several beds of a heated catalyst. The catalyst (an oxide of vanadium) speeds up the addition of oxygen to the sulphur dioxide. What type of reaction is this? When oxygen combines with sulphur dioxide, another oxide of sulphur called sulphur trioxide, SO_3, is formed.

$$2SO_2 + O_2 \rightarrow 2SO_3$$

The graph shows you how the amount of sulphur dioxide converted to sulphur trioxide changes with temperature. As the temperature increases, the reaction becomes faster but what happens to the yield of sulphur trioxide?

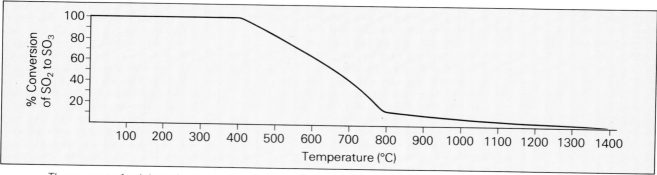

The amount of sulphur trioxide produced by the Contact process changes with temperature.

Making the acid

Sulphur trioxide reacts with water to form sulphuric acid as shown by the equation below.

$$SO_3 + H_2O \rightarrow H_2SO_4$$

At first sight it seems that all that has to be done is to dissolve the sulphur trioxide in water. However, if you try to dissolve sulphur trioxide in water, a great deal of heat is generated and a dense mist or fog of acid droplets is produced. This makes such a process impracticable. The problem can be overcome by dissolving sulphur trioxide into a mixture of 98% sulphuric acid and 2% water. The sulphur trioxide can safely react with the small amount of water present to form sulphuric acid.

Other sources of sulphur dioxide

Although sulphuric acid is a very useful chemical, the sulphur dioxide used to make it can cause harm to the environment. This is because if sulphur dioxide is released into the atmosphere it dissolves in rain water to form **acid rain**. This acid rain destroys plants and animals as well as causing damage to many building materials. Sulphur dioxide can be produced by the burning of fossil fuels such as coal, oil and natural gas which contain sulphur or sulphur compounds as impurities. Coal burning power stations, for example, emit more sulphur dioxide into the atmosphere than the chemical industry needs for the production of sulphur dioxide.

Coal fired power stations emit sulphur dioxide into the atmosphere.

1 Why do sulphuric acid plants have to be made from special building materials?

2 Sulphide ores can be heated in air to produce SO_2. Balance the equation below for the heating of zinc sulphide in air.

$$?ZnS + ?O_2 \rightarrow ?ZnO + ?SO_2$$

What type of reaction is this?

3 Look at the graph. What temperature do you think is the best for carrying out the contact process?

4 Some heat is produced when sulphur trioxide dissolves in 98% H_2SO_4 and 2% H_2O. In order to save energy, what do you think the heat could be used for?

5 Before the 1970s, 2% of the SO_2 produced by the contact process was lost to the atmosphere. Why is this no longer acceptable?

6 Where might future sources of SO_2 come from? What are the advantages of using this source for SO_2?

Electrolysis

Electrical conductors

The electrical energy that your TV uses is carried by **electricity** – the flow of electrons. Electricity flows through metals very easily. Such materials are good **electrical conductors**. They are, however, *chemically unchanged* when carrying electricity.

Electricity passes through electrical conductors as a flow of electrons all around a circuit. The metal wire remains chemically unchanged, but the compounds in the battery are chemically changed.

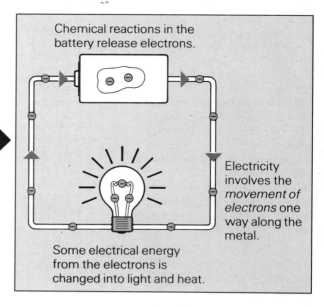

Chemical reactions in the battery release electrons.

Electricity involves the *movement of electrons* one way along the metal.

Some electrical energy from the electrons is changed into light and heat.

Electrolytic conductors

When melted, some compounds will conduct electricity. Rods called **electrodes** allow electrons to enter and leave such compounds. When electricity flows through such a compound (like lead bromide), some of the electrical energy *decomposes* (breaks down) the compound – this is *a chemical change*. The use of electricity to cause chemical change is called **electrolysis**. Compounds that can behave in this way are called **electrolytic conductors** or **electrolytes**.

Reactions at electrodes

Molten lead bromide is an ionic compound containing *free-moving* ions.

The positive ions are attracted to the cathode (which has a negative charge). The Pb^{2+} ion has 2 electrons *less* than the Pb atom. To change Pb^{2+} into a Pb atom, the lead ion must *gain* 2 electrons. These 2 electrons come from the surface of the cathode. This is represented by writing an **ionic equation**:

At the cathode: $Pb^{2+} + 2e^- \rightarrow Pb$

The negative ions are attracted to the anode. The Br^- ion has one electron *more* than the Br atom. To change Br^- into a Br atom, it must *lose* 1 electron. This electron is lost to the surface of the anode. The **ionic equation** for this reaction is:

At the anode: $Br^- \rightarrow Br + e^-$

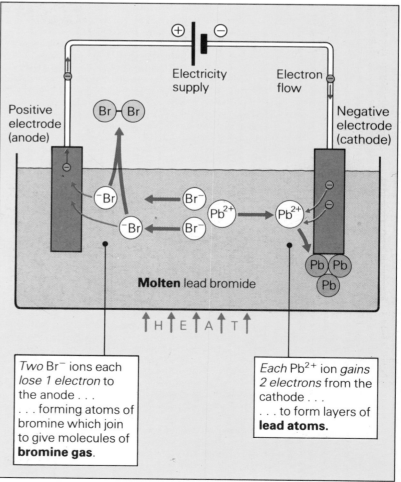

Electricity supply

Electron flow

Positive electrode (anode)

Negative electrode (cathode)

Molten lead bromide

H E A T

Two Br$^-$ ions each *lose 1 electron* to the anode . . .
. . . forming atoms of bromine which join to give molecules of **bromine gas**.

Each Pb^{2+} ion *gains 2 electrons* from the cathode . . .
. . . to form layers of **lead atoms.**

Aqueous electrolytes

If an ionic compound dissolves in water, it dissociates into free-moving ions (see 2.12). If carbon electrodes are placed in the solution, the **positive ions** are attracted to the *cathode*; the **negative ions** are attracted to the *anode*. The flow of electricity *through the solution* is caused by this *movement of ions* to the different electrodes. A chemical change takes place at the electrodes – so *aqueous solution of ionic compounds* are also **electrolytes**. However, with *aqueous* electrolytes, the water molecules can also take part in the chemical changes.

*Using reactivity tables, you can predict the **products** of electrolysis at the cathode (right) and anode (below).*

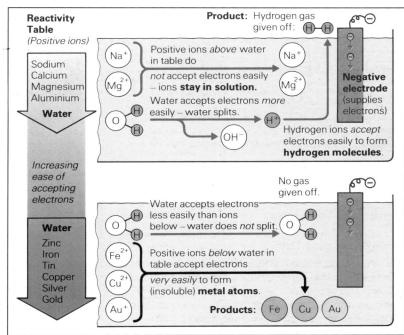

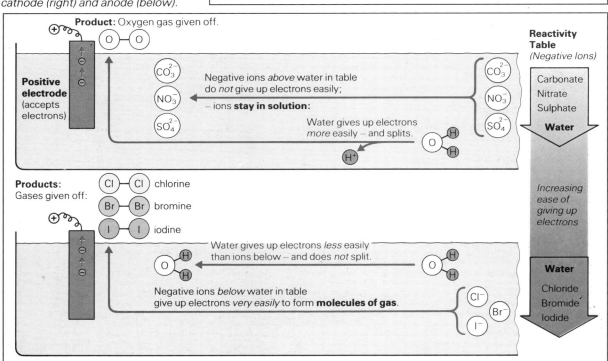

---

1 How does the conduction of electricity in metals differ from that in electrolytes?

2 The chemical process of **reduction** can be defined as the *addition of an electron*.
  a When molten lead bromide is electrolysed, does reduction take place at the anode or cathode?
  b **Oxidation** is the opposite of reduction. Define oxidation in terms of electron changes.

3 *Molten* sodium chloride (NaCl) is electrolysed industrially.
  a What forms at each electrode?
  b Write ionic equations for the reactions at each electrode.

4 Predict what is formed at each electrode when these *aqueous* solutions are electrolysed (using carbon electrodes):
  a magnesium bromide **b** copper chloride
  c sodium carbonate.

4.13 Electrolysis of salt water

More than just for flavour

Most common salt, the sort you put on your food, is found dissolved in the world's oceans. However, some occurs as solid rock salt. The largest deposits of rock salt in the United Kingdom are found on the Cheshire plain. Some of this salt dissolves in spring water to form natural underground streams of salt water or brine. People have used this brine for centuries as a source of salt to preserve food. During the Industrial Revolution salt became an important raw material for chemicals called alkalis which were needed for such things as soap and glass making.

Splitting up salt water

At the end of the last century it was known that electricity could be used to split substances up. This process is known as **electrolysis**. Common salt is sodium chloride, NaCl. Brine or, to give it its correct chemical name, sodium chloride solution, can be split up by electricity. One of the products obtained is an alkali called sodium hydroxide, NaOH. The other products are the gases chlorine, Cl_2, and hydrogen, H_2. The overall process can be described by the equation:

$$2NaCl + 2H_2O \xrightarrow{\text{electrolysis}} 2NaOH + Cl_2 + H_2$$

The photo shows you what happens when salt water containing universal indicator is electrolysed in the laboratory. What chemical properties of sodium hydroxide and chlorine are indicated by the colour of the indicator?

Some industrial processes

Although the electrolysis of brine might seem straightforward, there are problems. If the products are allowed to mix, the chlorine gas reacts with the sodium hydroxide to form sodium hypochlorite or household bleach. Industrial processes were developed to keep the products separate from each other. They all use the same electrolyte, brine, and produce the same products, but they keep them separate from each other in different ways.

The table shows you some facts about the three main processes. The Castner-Kellner process predominates in this country while the diaphragm cell is used mainly in the United States. More recently, the membrane cell is increasingly being used.

For centuries salt was obtained by heating brine in salt pans.

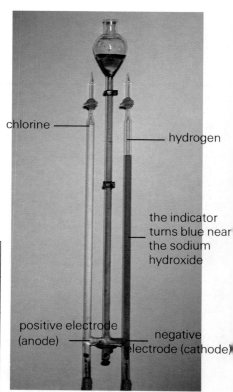
chlorine — hydrogen — the indicator turns blue near the sodium hydroxide — positive electrode (anode) — negative electrode (cathode)

Salt water can be electrolysed in the laboratory.

In Industry the electrolysis of brine can be carried out in three ways.

Type of cell	Castner-Kellner	Diaphragm	Membrane
Strength of NaOH	50%	12%	35%
Environmental problems	uses mercury, vapour is poisonous	uses asbestos which can cause cancer	no environmental problems
Special features	mercury is very expensive	diaphragm needs to be frequently replaced	needs very pure brine
Energy needs	uses the most energy	uses medium amount of energy	uses the least energy

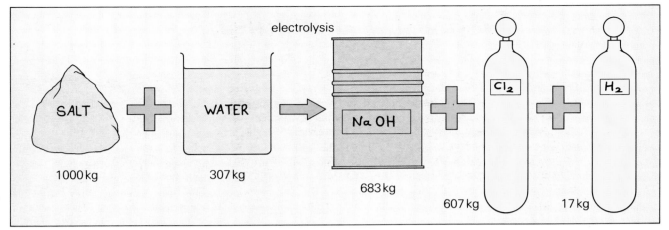

electrolysis

SALT 1000 kg + WATER 307 kg → NaOH 683 kg + Cl₂ 607 kg + H₂ 17 kg

The products from the electrolysis of brine are produced in fixed amounts.

Fixed amounts

At the turn of the century, the electrolysis of brine was used mainly to produce sodium hydroxide. This was needed by the alkali industry to satisfy increasing demand for such things as soap manufacture. However, the electrolysis of brine produces sodium hydroxide, chlorine and hydrogen in fixed amounts. This means you cannot produce more sodium hydroxide without also producing more chlorine and hydrogen. The diagram shows you how much of each product is produced when 1 tonne of salt water is electrolysed. Which product, chlorine or hydrogen, did the alkali industry find it more difficult to find users for?

Supply and demand

Hydrogen posed less problems for the alkali industry than chlorine. Not only was far less produced than chlorine but it could also be reacted with vegetable oils, such as groundnut oil, to make harder fats. These fats were first used as a raw material for soap making. They were later used to make margarine and for cooking. Any unused hydrogen could be burnt as an environmentally safe fuel – the product of burning was water.

Chlorine on the other hand is a poisonous gas. Any extra chlorine that was produced had to be stored – but what do you think happened if the storage facilities were full? Industry spent a long time developing new uses for chlorine and the demand for chlorine did not equal the demand for sodium hydroxide until the 1970s!

1900	1990
bleaching powder	PVC plastics
purifying water	solvents
poisonous gases	paints
	bleach
	purifying water

Many more uses for chlorine have been found. The uses are listed in order to demand.

1 What do the deposits of rock salt in Cheshire suggest it was covered by millions of years ago?

2 Look at the photo of the electrolysis of brine in the laboratory. What gas is collected at the **a** anode **b** cathode?

3 Look at the paragraph and the table about industrial processes.
   a what do the three processes have in common?
   b why do you think the membrane cell is increasingly being used?

4 Look at the data showing you the amounts of products produced by the electrolysis of brine. How much sodium hydroxide would be produced by the electrolysis of 4 tonnes of sodium chloride?

5 Why do you think the demand for soap increased during the Industrial Revolution?

6 Look at the data on the uses of chlorine.
   a how have the uses of the products changed?
   b why did the chemical industry also have to find new uses for sodium hydroxide?

95

4.14 *Extracting aluminium*

A very useful metal

You may be familiar with aluminium being used for chocolate wrapping paper and milk bottle tops. However, it is a very useful metal for all sorts of things. Compared to iron and steel, it is a very light metal. Weight for weight, it is a better conductor of electricity than copper and conducts heat well. Unlike iron, aluminium doesn't rust. It reacts with oxygen in the air to form an oxide layer and this oxide layer protects it from corrosion.

Aluminium is used in electrical transmission lines and aeroplanes.

A supply of bauxite

Aluminium is the most abundant metal on Earth. It makes up about 8% of the earth's crust. Rich deposits of aluminium, are only found in an ore known as **bauxite**. Large amounts of bauxite are found in Jamaica. These deposits are obtained by opencast mining. Before the aluminium can be extracted from the bauxite, it has to be purified further. The chemical process involved removes the major impurity, iron (III) oxide, as a 'red mud'. After mining and purifying the bauxite, not only are there ugly holes in the ground but also large red spoil heaps.

Electrolysis of molten alumina

The purified bauxite is a white powder called **alumina**. Chemically, it is pure aluminium oxide, Al_2O_3. Aluminium is extracted from the alumina by electrolysis. For the electrolysis to take place, the electrolyte needs to be molten (*see spread 4.12*). The melting point of alumina is very high – over 2000°C. This means large amounts of energy would be needed to melt it. If aluminium oxide is dissolved in molten cryolite the melting point is reduced to about 970°C. Cryolite is an aluminium ore with the chemical formula Na_3AlF_6. During electrolysis the aluminium oxide is decomposed by the electric current. Aluminium is formed at the negative electrode or cathode and oxygen gas at the positive electrode or anode.

Purified bauxite is shipped from Jamaica to smelters around the world.

In an aluminium smelter there are a large number of cells connected together.

The electrolytic cell

The electrolysis of alumina takes place in a cell similar to the one shown below. An aluminium smelting plant could have as many as 1000 such cells each capable of producing one tonne of aluminium a day!

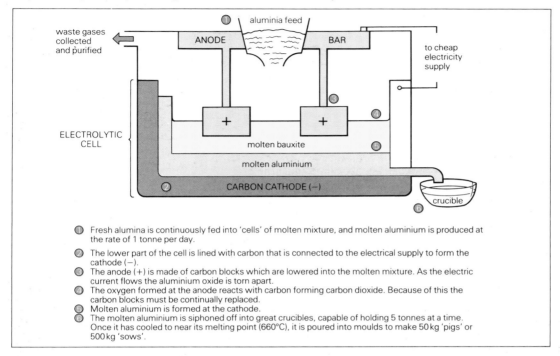

① Fresh alumina is continuously fed into 'cells' of molten mixture, and molten aluminium is produced at the rate of 1 tonne per day.

② The lower part of the cell is lined with carbon that is connected to the electrical supply to form the cathode (−).

③ The anode (+) is made of carbon blocks which are lowered into the molten mixture. As the electric current flows the aluminium oxide is torn apart.

④ The oxygen formed at the anode reacts with carbon forming carbon dioxide. Because of this the carbon blocks must be continually replaced.

⑤ Molten aluminium is formed at the cathode.

⑥ The molten aluminium is siphoned off into great crucibles, capable of holding 5 tonnes at a time. Once it has cooled to near its melting point (660°C), it is poured into moulds to make 50 kg 'pigs' or 500 kg 'sows'.

How much aluminium?

The aluminium industry depends on a cheap supply of electricity such as hydroelectric power. This is because vast quantities of electricity need to be consumed to produce large amounts of aluminium. The table opposite shows you how the mass of aluminium deposited at the cathode depends on the size of the current (a kA is a kiloampere or 1000 amperes). Look at the first two readings in the table. If the size of the current is doubled from 120 kA to 240 kA but the time for which the current flows is kept the same, then the mass of aluminium produced is doubled. What does the table show you about how the amount of aluminium produced depends on the time for which the current flows?

Current (kA)	Time (days)	Mass of aluminium (tonnes)
120	1	1
240	1	2
120	2	2

The mass of aluminium deposited at the cathode depends on the size of the current and the time for which it flows.

1 What properties of aluminium make it better than:
   a copper for electrical transmission lines
   b iron for aircraft construction?

2 As well as mining for bauxite, the other main money earner in Jamaica is tourism. What problems does mining cause for the tourist industry?

3 Why are aluminium smelting plants often situated near cheap sources of electricity and a deep water anchorage?

4 Look at the diagram of the electrolytic cell. What part of it needs to be constantly replaced?

5 During electrolysis, fluoride fumes are produced which can harm plants and animals. Where does the fluoride come from?

6 Look at the table. How much aluminium would be produced in four days by a current of 60 KA?

5.1 Natural cycles

Why aren't things used up?

The materials that make up your body were part of something else before you came into being! These materials have been on Earth since it was formed and have been used in many forms over the years. The materials aren't used up because they are constantly being recycled. The chemicals involved join together, then break down, only to reform again – the pattern of life is forever changing. The many factors that control these cycles interact in a moving, or **dynamic**, way to maintain the balance.

The water cycle

The water cycle is one of nature's important processes. Water is essential to life and it is maintained in balance through the cyclical interaction of the environment. ▼

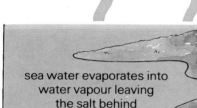

Below a certain temperature the invisible water vapour condenses into droplets that form clouds which can be seen.

water vapour rises by convection

energy from the sun

if droplets get too heavy they fall as rain

trees **transpire** and animals **respire** water vapour into the air

sea water evaporates into water vapour leaving the salt behind

without fresh water, land animals and plants would die

The carbon-oxygen cycle

Animals breathe in oxygen and breathe out carbon dioxide. Any animal trapped in an airtight place would soon die when the available oxygen was used up. The Earth itself is like an airtight place surrounded by empty space – so what stops this happening on Earth . . .?

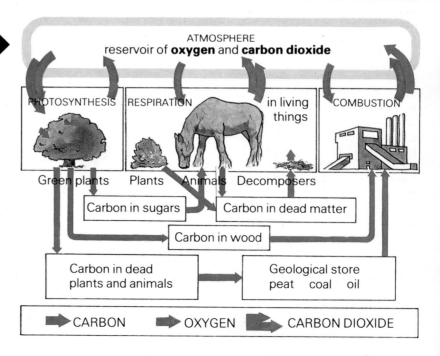

ATMOSPHERE
reservoir of **oxygen** and **carbon dioxide**

PHOTOSYNTHESIS   RESPIRATION   in living things   COMBUSTION

Green plants   Plants   Animals   Decomposers

Carbon in sugars   Carbon in dead matter

Carbon in wood

Carbon in dead plants and animals

Geological store
peat   coal   oil

CARBON   OXYGEN   CARBON DIOXIDE

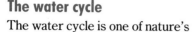

5 MATERIALS FROM THE EARTH

Maintaining the carbon/oxygen balance

By working in *opposite* directions, respiration and photosynthesis maintain a balanced atmosphere containing 20% oxygen but only 0.04% carbon dioxide. During **photosynthesis** plants give out ten times more oxygen than they take in during respiration. This surplus replaces all the oxygen used up during **combustion** (the burning of fuels) and animal **respiration**. By taking in carbon dioxide, the plants '*lock up*' carbon in the forms of starch and cellulose. Such carbon is not immediately available for recycling. Animals which eat the starch release the carbon as carbon dioxide during respiration. Any carbon 'locked up' in plants and animals when they die is recycled by the respiratory action of the **decomposers**. The more woody cellulose is slower to rot and may be compressed down into peat and finally into coal. Some carbon dioxide combines with calcium to form sea shells and these shells left on the sea bed can become compressed over time to form chalk.

Decaying forests no longer recycle gases into the air. The carbon becomes locked up in coal and peat.

Early days

The water and the carbon-oxygen cycles have not always been in process. When the Earth was formed the atmosphere was made up of mainly **methane** and **ammonia** gases. The temperature was so great that any free oxygen reacted with these two gases to form **carbon dioxide**, **water vapour** and unreactive **nitrogen**. When the Earth cooled enough, water fell as rain, forming rivers and seas – this helped to cool the Earth even more quickly. The carbon dioxide was then used by the first plants to produce **food** by photosynthesis – which released **oxygen** into the air. Once the oxygen level was high enough, animal life began. For the last 200 million years, photosynthesis and respiration have maintained a *constant and necessary balance* between carbon dioxide and oxygen in the atmosphere – until now!

In the last 200 years, millions of tonnes of coal and oil has been burnt for fuel. This has added much more carbon dioxide to the atmosphere. We humans are now upsetting the cycle by burning coal and oil faster than they are produced. Over the same period, vast numbers of trees in the rain forests have been cut down. These trees, through their photosynthesis, used to remove enormous quantities of carbon dioxide from the air and replace it with oxygen. But again people have interfered and upset the natural cycle on a large scale. As a result there is currently an increasing level of carbon dioxide in the atmosphere which may cause increased temperature due to the '**greenhouse**' effect – which may in turn affect the water cycle by altering the weather patterns.

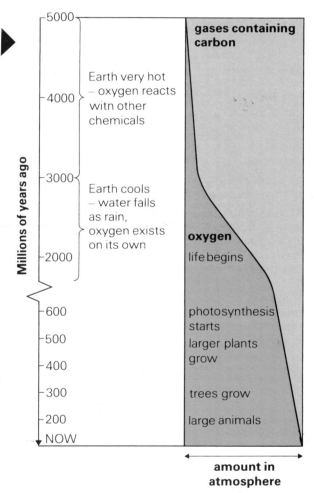

Millions of years ago

gases containing carbon

5000

4000 — Earth very hot – oxygen reacts with other chemicals

3000 — Earth cools – water falls as rain, oxygen exists on its own

oxygen

2000 — life begins

600 — photosynthesis starts

500 — larger plants grow

400

300 — trees grow

200 — large animals

NOW

amount in atmosphere

Large farms often spray fertiliser from the air onto the land.

---

1 Energy is needed to 'run' these natural cycles. What supplies this energy and what process does it start in
   a the water cycle
   b the carbon/oxygen cycle?

2 Why did the level of carbon dioxide in the air begin to fall
   a gradually, about 600 million years ago?
   b rapidly, about 250 million years ago?

Bring on the clouds

The Earth's atmosphere

The Earth is surrounded by a thin transparent 'shell' gases held by the Earth's gravity. The shell is known as the **atmosphere** or, more commonly, as just 'air'.

You live at the bottom of this shell of air – indeed you could not live without it. The atmosphere is many kilometres thick – the whole shell of air has a mass of many million tonnes. The air near the ground is compressed by the weight of all the air above it. The weight causes the air to exert a pressure on everything around it. At sea level, this is equivalent to 1 kilogram pressing down (i.e. a force of 10 N) on each square centimetre.

This **air pressure** is usually measured in Pascals ($Pa = N/m^2$) or millibars. At sea level, the air pressure is 1.013×10^5 Pa (1013 millibars).

Exploring the atmosphere

People explore the atmosphere by sending up balloons and artificial satellites. These carry instruments that record, for example, the temperature and pressure at different heights.

Such investigations show that air pressure and density decrease with height as the weight of air above gets less.

At 150 kilometres high, air pressure and density are very low, and eventually the atmosphere merges into space. The temperature of the air also varies with height, but in a much less uniform way. The way the temperature changes with height is used to divide the atmosphere up into 'layers'.

Layers of air

In the layer of air closest to the ground, the **troposphere**, the temperature decreases with height, dropping steadily by 6.5°C/km. This is why you can find ice forming at the equator – if you are at the top of very tall mountains!

Heating occurs in the **stratosphere** because a form of oxygen called **ozone** absorbs some of the energy in the Sun's ultraviolet rays.

The temperature falls in the **mesophere**, to rise again in the **ionosphere**, where other gases absorb energy from the Sun's rays.

At sea level, you have the weight of a vast column of air pressing on you. ▼

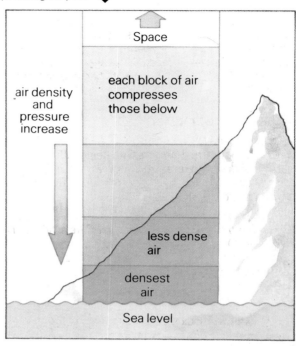

height above ground	temperature of air	layer of atmosphere
150 km	+150°C	
	+100°C	**ionosphere** – temperature *rises* with height (caused by harshest radiation from Sun)
80 km	−50°C	
		mesosphere – temperature *falls* with height (air absorbs little energy from sunlight)
50 km	+80°C	
		stratosphere – temperature *rises* with height (caused by ozone absorbing u.v. light)
20 km	−50°C	*tropopause* (no convection can pass through)
10 km		**troposphere** – temperature *falls* with height (temperature gradient allows convection to occur)
0 km	+20°C	

Moisture in the air

Energy from the Sun warms the surface of the Earth, which heats the air near the ground. This warm air rises in a **convection current** up through the troposphere.

The rising warm air gradually loses heat energy to the surrounding cooler air. Water vapour in the warm air also loses heat until it condenses as tiny droplets of water, forming a mist or **cloud**. The temperature at which a mist forms is called the **dewpoint**. If the air is cooled further, the water droplets become so large they fall as **rain**.

The lid on the weather

Warm air rises in the troposphere because in this layer temperature *decreases* with height. But in the stratosphere, temperature *increases* with height. So convection currents cannot usually move from the troposphere into the stratosphere.

The cloud-carrying convection currents are trapped *beneath* the **tropopause**, which acts like a 'lid' on the weather. Only very violent convection currents, such as those from a volcano, can break through the tropopause and rise into the stratosphere.

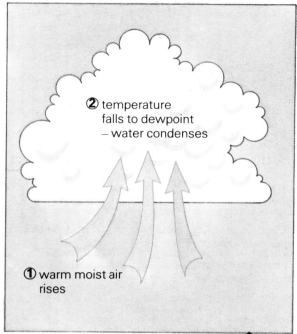

Invisible water vapour in the rising moist air condenses to form clouds.

Mountains in the rain

In this country, winds often blow from the west, bringing wet, warm air mainly from over the large area of Atlantic Ocean. These winds push the wet air up over any mountains in their path.

As the air rises the temperature may drop to the dewpoint. Then clouds will form and rain may fall over the mountains.

Mountains, as well as convection currents, can cause clouds to form.

Types of cloud

The shape of a cloud depends on *how* it is formed, the *height* at which it is formed and the *speed of the wind*.

Each shape or type of cloud is given a name. The fluffy, cotton-wool clouds are called **cumulus**, while layered clouds stretched out by the wind are known as **stratus**.

Cirro- is used to describe high clouds, and **alto-** is used for middle-level clouds. So, for example, alto-cumulus is a medium-level cumulus and cirro-stratus is a high-level stratus.

1 Why do people find it difficult to breathe at the top of high mountains?

2 What happens when the dewpoint temperature falls to ground level?

3 At any time, bases of clouds are all about the same height above the ground. Why?

4 Do winds from the east cause as much rain on the mountains in Britain as winds from the west? Give reasons for your answers.

5 Passenger aircraft fly in the stratosphere rather than the troposphere. Suggest reasons for this.

5.3 What's the weather like?

Driven by the Sun

Conditions in the atmosphere around you – the **weather** – may be wet or dry, hot or cold, sunny or cloudy. This will affect what you do, the clothes you wear and even the food you eat.

The weather can change rapidly. Accurate forecasts of the weather are important for many industries (such as ice-cream manufacturers), farmers and transport, particularly shipping. What causes the weather and its variations?

The weather systems of the world are powered by the Sun. Because the Earth is a sphere, the Sun's rays fall on a *smaller* area (and are more *concentrated*) around the equator than at the poles. This uneven heating causes movement of the air – the **winds**. Winds transfer energy from the warmer to the cooler regions of the Earth.

The Sun evaporates water from the oceans and seas. The rain that falls on you may have been evaporated here in the Caribbean Sea and carried to Britain by the wind.

The Earth's winds

The air moves in fairly steady patterns near the equator and the poles. Warm air rises in huge convection currents over the equator. It then falls back at latitudes of about 30°.

Air rushes across the surface towards the equator to replace the rising air. Similarly, the cold air above the poles falls and is replaced by warmer air drawn from lower latitudes. Between these two huge convection currents, no steady patterns form.

This is because high in the atmosphere very strong winds known as the **jet-stream** flow from west to east. These disturb the air, resulting in the unsettled weather we experience in the UK.

The great convection currents would flow north or south if the Earth were still. But the Earth keeps spinning to the east! Even if the air flows directly south, when you compare it to the point on the Earth where it started from, the air will have moved south *and* west.

Why should this be so? On any spinning sphere, the further the surface is from the axis, the faster it spins. So at the equator, the Earth spins *fastest*. North of the equator, air and Earth spin eastwards more *slowly*. As this air flows south to the faster-spinning equator, it can't 'keep up' with the eastward spin at the equator. When it reaches the equator, the Earth has spun round further. Compared with the point on the Earth where it started from, the air will have moved south *and* west.

All the Earth's winds are deflected away from north–south by the Earth's spin.

Air pressure and wind

The rising and falling air causes differences in air pressure. Falling air produces a *high* pressure at ground level, and the air spreads out. Rising air leaves a *low* pressure at ground level and air is drawn in.

Air always moves from areas of high pressure to areas of low pressure creating winds. The spin of the Earth causes these winds to swirl or spiral around high and low-pressure areas.

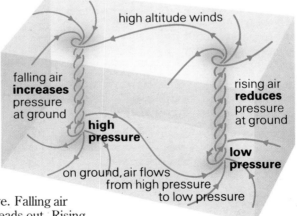

In the northern hemisphere, the winds flow anti-clockwise around low-pressure areas and clockwise around high-pressure areas.

Plotting the weather

Weather maps show where areas of high and low pressure are situated. They do this using **isobars** – lines joining places where the pressure at ground level is the same. Just as contour lines on ordinary maps indicate steep slopes – so if isobars are close together, the pressure differences in that area are great. The *closer* the isobars, the greater the pressure difference – and the *stronger* the winds.

As winds spiral in towards low-pressure areas, the air they carry may be warmer or cooler than the air it replaces. Where such a *change* of air is taking place is called a **front**.

Change makes rain

Warm air is less dense than cool air. When warm air is blown into replace cooler air, the warmer lighter air is pushed up and over the cooler heavier air. This is known as a **warm front**. When a **cold front** occurs, the cold air moving in is pushed *underneath* the existing warm air.

As the warm air is forced upwards, it cools, and moisture condenses out and falls as rain. Bad weather is associated with the changes that take place when fronts move. Once the original block of air has been completely replaced the weather is usually settled and fine. It is the *change* of air that causes rain.

Weather and climate

Although the weather can vary from day to day, over a number of years the weather of an area follows a pattern. The *average* weather of an area over many years is called its **climate**. The climate of an area affects people in many ways – particularly the food they can grow. Farmers in Britain plant crops and keep livestock suited to our temperate climate.

Until recently, only natural changes could affect the climate. For example, the Sun's energy fluctuates slightly over the years and this *may* result in fluctuations in climate. Now our industries are releasing carbon dioxide into the atmosphere, which is trapping more of the Sun's energy. This may lead to serious climate changes.

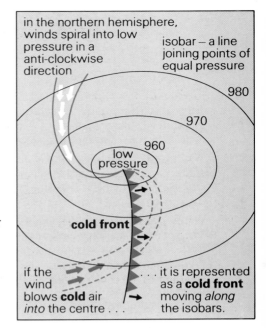

in the northern hemisphere, winds spiral into low pressure in a anti-clockwise direction

isobar – a line joining points of equal pressure

980
970
960
low pressure

cold front

if the wind blows **cold** air *into* the centre . . .

. . . it is represented as a **cold front** moving *along* the isobars.

Low pressure areas are called cyclones and high pressure areas are anticyclones.

A warm front moving in brings rain – until the warm air has replaced the cold air.

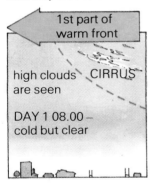

1st part of warm front

high clouds are seen   CIRRUS

DAY 1 08.00 – cold but clear

2nd part of warm front

ALTO CUMULUS

DAY 1 20.00 – getting cloudy

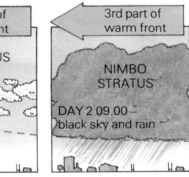

3rd part of warm front

NIMBO STRATUS

DAY 2 09.00 – black sky and rain

Last part of warm front

FAIR WEATHER CUMULUS

DAY 2 16.00 – warm and bright

1
a Give four examples of industries which might need accurate forecasts of the weather.
b What provides energy to create the destructive winds in hurricanes?

2 All winds are named after the direction they blow *from*. Name the Earth's winds shown in the diagram on the opposite page.

3 In the northern hemisphere, water runs down the plughole in an anti-clockwise direction. Suggest why.

4 How does a front cause rain?

5 When a high-pressure area has its centre over Sweden, we get a heat wave in summer or a cold spell in winter. Suggest reasons why.

6 Carbon dioxide traps the Sun's energy through the '**greenhouse effect**'.
a Find out about the greenhouse effect.
b Predict how this might affect the climate in Britain and the food we can grow.

5.4 Eroding the rocks

Weatherbeaten rocks

From the day the first drop of rain hit the Earth's crust, **weathering** (wearing down of rocks) and **erosion** (the carrying away of weathered parts of rocks) started changing the landscape.

Water evaporated by the Sun eventually falls as rain, snow or hail. The water that falls on land may soak into the ground, flow as streams and rivers, freeze to ice or even form 'rivers' of ice called **glaciers**.

Water in all its forms is the main agent of weathering. The pounding sea can wear away the solid rock of cliffs. Water expands as it freezes, and if ice forms in rock crevices it can split the rock. These are examples of *physical* weathering. Rocks can also be weathered *chemically*, mainly by weak acids in the water reacting with the rock.

Erosion transports away pieces of rock broken away by weathering. Often such rock is broken down further by other rocks as it is being carried away (e.g. in rivers).

Repeated weathering eventually breaks down rock into small particles of **sand** or **clay**. These particles gradually settle out as deposits on river-beds, banks and beaches.

U-shaped valley carved by glacier – and *containing a glacier.*

Chemical attack

As rain falls, **carbon dioxide** in the air combines with the water to form a **weak acid**. Some of the substances in rocks, such as the calcium carbonate in **limestone**, dissolve in the slightly acidic rainwater. This happens gradually – for example, it has taken centuries for rain to eat away the faces of limestone statues on old cathedrals in Britain.

The process is speeded up by industrial pollutants, such as the gas **sulphur dioxide** which dissolves to produce sulphuric acid. This type of **acid rain** wears away more quickly limestone statues, buildings and natural rock faces.

In limestone areas, water transforms the landscape through chemical attack and the rubbing action of loosened stones carried along by the water. ▼

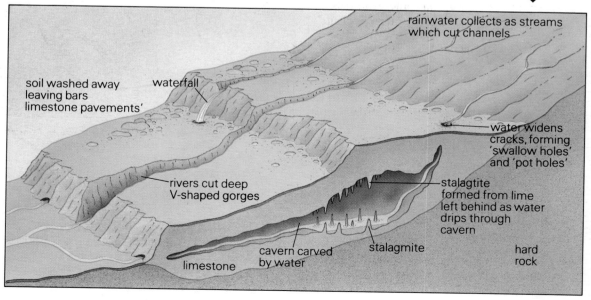

rainwater collects as streams which cut channels

soil washed away leaving bars limestone pavements'

waterfall

water widens cracks, forming 'swallow holes' and 'pot holes'

rivers cut deep V-shaped gorges

stalagtite formed from lime left behind as water drips through cavern

cavern carved by water

stalagmite

hard rock

limestone

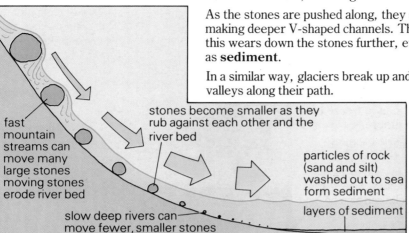

As a river flows from the hills to the sea, the slope of the river bed becomes gentler and the water flows more slowly. ▼

fast mountain streams can move many large stones moving stones erode river bed

stones become smaller as they rub against each other and the river bed

particles of rock (sand and silt) washed out to sea form sediment

slow deep rivers can move fewer, smaller stones

layers of sediment

From the river to the sea

Rain collects on hills in streams which later combine to form rivers. Up in the hills, fast-moving waters sweep up the pieces of rock (stones) washed into them, including those loosened by chemical attack.

As the stones are pushed along, they scratch away at the rock below making deeper V-shaped channels. The moving stones hit each other and this wears down the stones further, eventually depositing tiny particles as **sediment**.

In a similar way, glaciers break up and transport rocks, carving **U**-shaped valleys along their path.

Any steep slope tends to be eroded by flowing water. ▼

Other weatherers

Although water and ice are the main breakers of rocks, there are other weathering agents.

Rocks expand as they get hotter and contract as they cool. In desert areas with extremes of **temperature** between day and night, frequent expansion and contraction can *shatter* the rock. **Wind** carrying small particles of sand and grit can carve rocks, in the way that sandblasting is used to clean the faces of buildings.

Even **plants** can cause weathering – their roots grow into crevices in rocks, splitting the rocks apart.

Vanishing soil

Over thousands of years, weathering and erosion slowly change the landscape, and may expose valuable minerals. This also helps to produce a fertile layer covering the rocks – **topsoil**.

The tiny particles of clay, sand and other materials formed by weathering provide all the minerals plants need. The type and amount of plants that can grow depend partly on the quality and depth of the topsoil.

Plant roots, particularly the large root systems of trees, **bind** the fine particles of soil together. When people clear away trees, rainwater or wind can carry the soil away leaving barren rock. The soil which took so long to form can be eroded in only a few years.

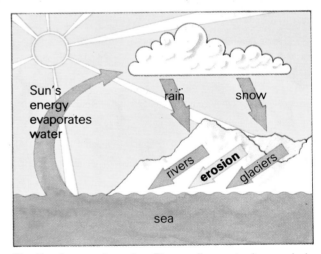

Sun's energy evaporates water

rain

snow

rivers

erosion

glaciers

sea

The Sun 'powers' erosion. The eroding water is recycled but the eroded rocks and soil move one way – downwards.

1
  a Give two examples of physical weathering.
  b In chemical weathering, what would happen if the rainwater became even more acid than it is now?

2
  a The estuary of a river (where the river meets the sea) often **silts** up. Explain where the silt has come from.
  b If you found a rock on the shore with sharp edges, what type of weathering might have caused them?

3 Farmers who want to grow crops on steep hillsides often build wide 'steps' or **terraces** in the hill. Suggest reasons for this.

4 Erosion and weathering have been moving soil and rocks downhill for millions of years. Suggest a hypothesis to explain why all the hills have not worn away.

5.5 *Looking at soil*

The 'living' soil

The soil is a habitat for many small and even microscopic creatures. It has been estimated that there are more living things in a spadeful of soil than there are humans on the Earth! The bacteria and small animals play an important part in decomposing dead material and returning its nutrients to the soil. The type of soil and the nutrients it contains affects the sorts of plants that can flourish in it. The sorts of plants that grow, in turn, affect the sorts of animals that choose that habitat.

What is soil?

Soil is made from **rock** which has been broken down in to tiny pieces over the course of time by the action of flowing water, ice, temperature changes, rain, or any combination of these factors. The type of soil formed reflects the nature of the parent rock. A sandstone will form sandy soil. Water can, however, carry soil a long way from where it was formed. Minerals dissolved from the rocks by acid rain enrich the soil and provide many of the nutrients needed by plants.

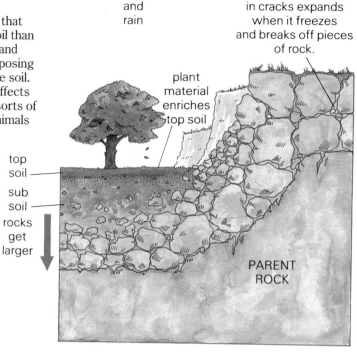

wind and rain

Water collected in cracks expands when it freezes and breaks off pieces of rock.

plant material enriches top soil

top soil

sub soil

rocks get larger

PARENT ROCK

Looking closely at soil

If a sample of soil is well shaken in water then allowed to settle, the range of particle sizes can be seen in what is called a **soil profile**. The decaying pieces of plant material that float to the top are called **humus**. ▼

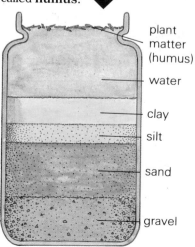

plant matter (humus)

water

clay

silt

sand

gravel

dry soil in

stones 2.00 mm+

coarse sand 2 – 0.2 mm

fine sand 0.2 – 0.02 mm

silt 0.02 – 0.002 mm

clay 0.002 mm −

▲

If the soil sample is dried and then shaken through a series of sieves, each with a finer mesh, then the soil can be separated into a range of particles of different sizes.

Type of soil

Sandy soils have large, odd-shaped particles which cannot pack close together. This leaves large air spaces. Water can quickly drain past the large particles. ▼

Light and easy to work.

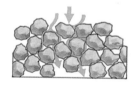

Clay particles are very fine like talcum powder and pack closely together so any air spaces are small. Water drains past the particles slowly and tends to cling to the fine clay particles. ▼

Heavy and hard to work.

Live contents

Apart from the microscopic bacteria and algae, the soil contains many small animals. These include insects, centipedes, mites and worms. Some of these are 'burrowers' – they tunnel through the soil thus helping to get air into the soil. The action of earthworms (in pulling leaves down into their burrows for food) increases the humus content. Worms take in soil to help them digest their food. When this soil is released as a worm cast, it is much finer.

Dead contents

The amount of humus in the soil is very important. Humus in sandy soils helps to *retain* the water and prevent the soil draining too quickly. In clay soils the humus *breaks up* the tightly packed clumps of clay into smaller crumbs.

Chemical contents

Soil also varies depending on its mineral content. Chalk soils are often **alkaline** due to the lime content. Decaying leaves can make a soil **acid**.

	Weight of earthworms (kg per hectare)
pasture	500 – 1500
deciduous wood	400 – 700
arable farmland	20 – 800
coniferous woodland	50 – 200

You can judge how many worms you may find in a typical soil from this table. Why do you think there are so few earthworms in coniferous forests?

This soil has developed on top of chalk rock.

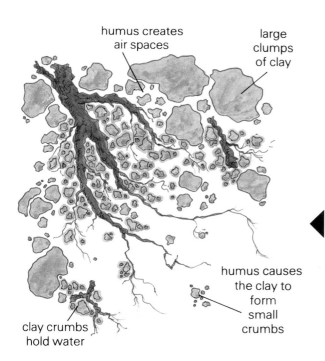

humus creates air spaces

large clumps of clay

humus causes the clay to form small crumbs

clay crumbs hold water

Good growing soil

Good growing soil must contain the **water** that plants need to absorb through their roots. The soil should also have enough of the **minerals** and **nutrients** that plants need for healthy growth. Good soil must also contain air spaces, since the roots get the **oxygen** for respiration from these spaces.

If a soil becomes water logged then there will be no oxygen available for the plant and it will die. Eventually even the bacteria which rot the plant material will die. As a result the dead plants in such soil rot slowly. Such soil becomes very acid and is called '**peaty**' because it contains so much half-rotted plant material.

1. Describe how you would set about estimating the numbers of small animals, such as centipedes found in an area of soil.

2. Gardeners allow dead plant material to rot on a compost heap and then spread it on the garden. Give two reasons why they do this.

3. Can you suggest why the soil in a field on an arable farm contains so few worms at certain times?

4. You might think that the abundance of leaves in a deciduous wood would attract many worms. Can you think why this is *not* the case?

5.6 Recycling rocks

Rock types

The Earth's crust is made up of many kinds of rock which differ in their hardness and other properties. The properties of rocks depend partly on *how* they were formed. Rocks are classified into three *groups* – **igneous**, **sedimentary** and **metamorphic** – according to their origin.

Igneous rocks were once molten rocks. Temperature increases with depth in the Earth. Below the crust, some rock melts to form **magma** (molten rock). This magma may be forced up into the crust, forming a **pluton** – or it may surface as **lava** from a volcano. On cooling, crystals grow in the magma – and it solidifies. The *type* and *size* of crystals in igneous rock depend how *quickly* the magma cools – and on the chemical composition of the magma.

Igneous rocks are very hard and some of the crystals they contain, such as diamonds, are the hardest materials of all.

Sedimentary rocks are formed from grains of eroded rock (silt, sand and so on) or the undecomposed parts of plants and animals. These sediments settle in horizontal layers, usually under water. The older layers, buried under newer layers, are slowly *compressed* into sedimentary rock. For example, mud is compressed into **mudstone**, and the remains of tiny shellfish form the white rock, **chalk**.

If a sedimentary rock continues to be buried *deeper* in the crust, it is subject to higher temperatures and pressures. Although the rock does not fully melt, later small crystals form on cooling. The great pressure of the weight of rock above causes the crystals to form in parallel planes or **bands**.

The *changed* rock is known as **metamorphic rock**. For example, sedimentary mudstone can be changed to metamorphic **slate**, and chalk to **marble**.

Metamorphic rocks are usually harder and more resistant to erosion than sedimentary rocks.

Using rocks

Rocks are quarried or mined for the **minerals** they contain, and also for use as **building materials**. The choice of rock for building depends on the properties of the rock and the cost of quarrying it. Harder rock is longer lasting, but it is more difficult (and so more expensive) to work.

Deep in the crust, sedimentary sandstone changes to metamorphic quartzite.

Basalt contains small *crystals because it is formed from lava which cools* rapidly *on the surface of the Earth.*

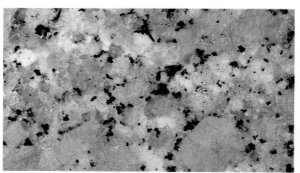

Granite is formed by slow *cooling in a pluton, allowing* large *crystals to form.*

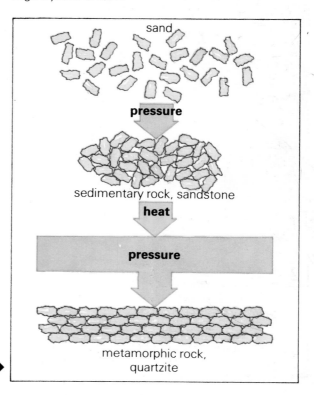

Rock type	Relative properties			
	crush strength	impact strength	wear on tyres in dry	wear on tyres in wet
Flint (igneous)	9	24	24	26
Gabbro (igneous)	7	31	26	22
Schist (metamorphic)	14	15	20	16
Quartzite (metamorphic)	28	20	26	24
Sandstone (sedimentary)	9	16	24	12
Limestone (sedimentary)	2	0.5	18	1

This table shows some properties of rocks used to make roads. Compare the properties of sandstone and quartzite (metamorphic sandstone) and suggest reasons for the differences.

The rock cycle shows sandstone being formed and recycled as sedimentary rock – Quartzite – (metamorphic rock) and some melts as magma. The rocks get cooler as the diagram moves from bottom to top.

The rock cycle

Over millions of years, one rock type can gradually change into another.

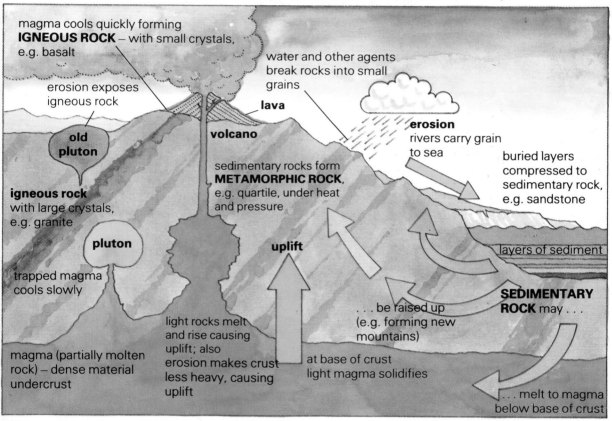

magma cools quickly forming **IGNEOUS ROCK** – with small crystals, e.g. basalt

erosion exposes igneous rock

water and other agents break rocks into small grains

lava

volcano

old pluton

erosion
rivers carry grain to sea

sedimentary rocks form **METAMORPHIC ROCK**, e.g. quartile, under heat and pressure

buried layers compressed to sedimentary rock, e.g. sandstone

igneous rock with large crystals, e.g. granite

pluton

uplift

layers of sediment

trapped magma cools slowly

light rocks melt and rise causing uplift; also erosion makes crust less heavy, causing uplift

. . . be raised up (e.g. forming new mountains)

SEDIMENTARY ROCK may . . .

magma (partially molten rock) – dense material undercrust

at base of crust light magma solidifies

. . . melt to magma below base of crust

1
a What is a pluton?
b Would you expect to find larger crystals in lava or in a pluton?

2 Explain the following:
a Slate (a metamorphic rock) can easily be broken into thin sheets;
b Plugs of volcanic lava are often left standing as vertical columns.

3 Sedimentary rocks are recycled by nature in three ways. Describe the changes that take place during each of these.

4
a Display the information in the table above in a way that highlights the different properties of the rocks used for roads.
b Which of the three main types of rock:
  i) cause least wear on tyres in the dry;
  ii) are the hardest to crush;
  iii) the hardest to crack;
c A road-maker wants a surface that will resist accidental damage and give good road-holding in the wet, yet will not be too damaging to tyres in the dry. Suggest a mixture of rocks for the road-maker to use.

5.7   The restless Earth

Below the surface

According to the rock cycle theory (*see 5.6*), partially molten magma will form in certain places below the crust. How did scientists gather evidence for this theory?

We live on the surface of the crust and it seems firm and calm. Yet the evidence of activity below the surface is only too apparent in some parts of the world – areas with volcanoes and earthquakes.

Volcanoes

Deep in the crust, rocks are pushed down by the weight of rocks above. The higher temperatures further down in the Earth melt the lower rocks and they form partially molten magma. This magma is less dense than surrounding rocks and so rises up towards the crust. The pressure of surrounding rocks, and from gases in the magma, forces it to rise up through any areas of weakness in the crust. If the area of weakness reaches to the surface, a volcano is born! A **volcano** is an opening or vent through which magma reaches the surface.

Gases trapped in the magma eject it from the volcano as **lava**. Depending on the pressure of the gases, this may be a gentle or violent process. During an explosive **eruption**, hot ash and rocks may fall over a wide area causing serious damage and loss of life.

Other evidence of Earth movements – earthquakes – can have even more catastrophic effects.

Volcanoes change the landscape forming hills (also known as volcanoes), plateaux and depressions. ▶

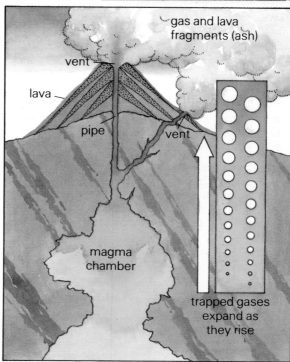

Some volcanoes build up a layered core of lava and ash. ▶

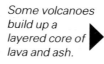

Would you live in San Francisco?

Earthquakes

During the evening rush-hour on 17 October 1989, an earthquake hit San Francisco. Over 300 people died as bridges, motorway and buildings collapsed. Ever since the great San Francisco quake of 1906 people had been waiting for 'the big one' – but although it was expected, it wasn't accurately predicted.

San Francisco lies on the *San Andreas fault* – a place where two great pieces of the Earth's crust are trying to move in opposite directions. The friction between the two blocks holds them together. But when the pressure below them becomes too great, they move past each other.

Frequently, a block slips a few metres resulting in smaller tremors. But during this recent quake, slippage occured over a 56 km length of the fault, releasing as much energy as an atomic bomb explosion!

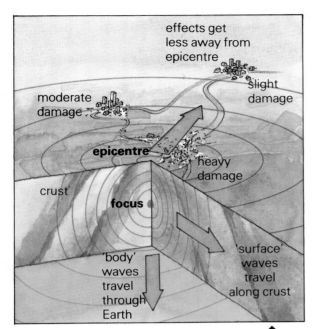

During a major earthquake, the surface waves ▲ cause extensive damage.

Predicting disaster

Before a volcanic eruption, there is increased activity in smaller vents and the temperature in the volcano rises. These signs may be detected by special satellites orbiting the Earth.

As a result, volcanic eruptions *can* often be predicted. When Mount St. Helens erupted in 1980 everyone except the photographers and scientists had been evacuated! Unfortunately, earthquakes are more difficult to predict. They may be preceded by small tremors – or none at all. Any shock waves are detected by **seismometers** at stations all round the world.

Locating earthquakes

Body waves travel faster along a more direct route than surface waves. So there is a time interval between the arrival of body and surface waves at a seismometer station. This time interval, and others, indicate the *distance* from the station to the epicentre.

The distance of the epicentre from at least three stations can be used to locate the epicentre.

1 How do volcanoes and earthquakes provide evidence for the rock cycle theory?

2 a What pushes lava out of a volcano?
  b Cooling lava can plug the vent of a volcano, making it appear inactive. What could happen if magma continues to be forced up to the base of the plug?

Shock waves

The point where the slippage occurs between the blocks is the **focus** of the earthquake. This may be close to the surface or deep underground. The point on the surface directly above the focus is called the **epicentre**. The movement sends **shock waves** along the crust (**surface** waves) and through the Earth (**body** waves).

The damage an earthquake can cause depends on the energy released. This is measured on the **Richter scale** – named after the scientist who first classified the effect of earthquakes. You would scarcely notice an earthquake measuring 2 on the Richter scale. Anything over 7 is a major earthquake capable of destroying buildings. Each year throughout the world about 20 earthquakes 'score' more than 7 on the Richter scale.

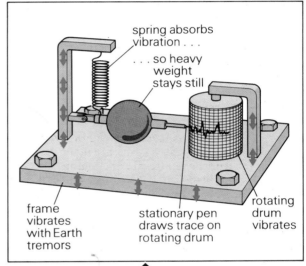

A simple seismometer ▲

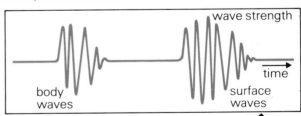

Shock waves recorded by a seismometer – a ▲ **seismograph**. The larger the time interval between certain waves, the further away the epicentre.

3 Explain the difference between the focus of an earthquake and its epicentre.

4 a How can shock waves be used to direct aid to earthquake disasters?
  b In 1988 in Armenia, Russia 25 000 people were killed by an earthquake measuring 6.9 on the Richter Scale. Compare this with the San Francisco quake and suggest reasons why fewer people died in the Californian one.

5.8 *The inside story*

Revealing the Earth's structure

We can observe the Earth's atmosphere and surface, and people have drilled or mined about 13 km down in the crust. But the centre of the Earth is about 6370 km down. How can we find out what the inside of the Earth is like? Although there is no *direct* information, the shock waves of earthquakes (and underground explosions) reveal clues about the Earth's structure.

Shock waves, like many other waves, can be bent or *refracted*. They travel at different speeds in materials of different density, and the waves are refracted as they pass from one material into another.

By detecting the body waves that have passed through the Earth, a picture of the inside of the Earth can be built up. This suggests that the Earth is made up of layers of different density. The waves also reveal the **state** of the layers – whether they are solid or liquid.

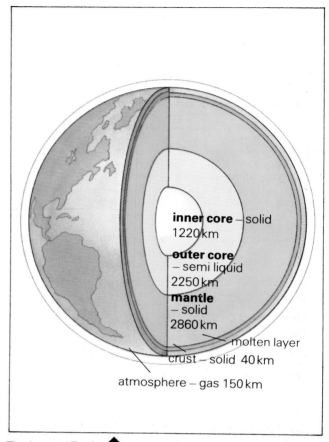

inner core – solid
1220 km
outer core – semi liquid
2250 km
mantle – solid
2860 km
molten layer
crust – solid 40 km
atmosphere – gas 150 km

The layered Earth ▲

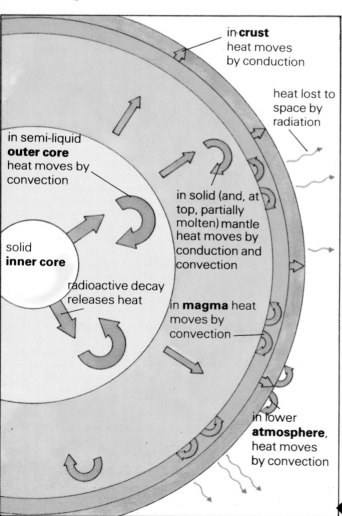

in **crust**
heat moves by conduction

heat lost to space by radiation

in semi-liquid **outer core** heat moves by convection

in solid (and, at top, partially molten) **mantle** heat moves by conduction and convection

solid **inner core**

radioactive decay releases heat

in **magma** heat moves by convection

in lower **atmosphere**, heat moves by convection

Hotting up

If you go down a very deep mine you find that temperature increases with depth in the Earth. Near the surface, the temperature rises between 10 and 20°C for every kilometre you go down. This change in temperature shows that much heat is released from deep inside the Earth.

There is no way of measuring temperatures below the deepest mine, so scientists make various assumptions. For example, they assume that the rate of heat loss is greater through the crust than lower in the Earth. This leads them to suggest that the temperature at the centre is about 5000°C.

Since heat is being lost from the Earth, it should be cooling down – but the rate of heat loss near the surface remains steady. So the Earth must be *producing* heat to make up for this loss. One hypothesis suggests that this heat is provided by natural radioactive materials decaying near the centre of the Earth.

◀ *Heat is transferred from the centre of the Earth to space by conduction, convection and radiation.*

112   **YOU CAN READ MORE ABOUT RADIOACTIVE DECAY ON SPREAD 3.10.**

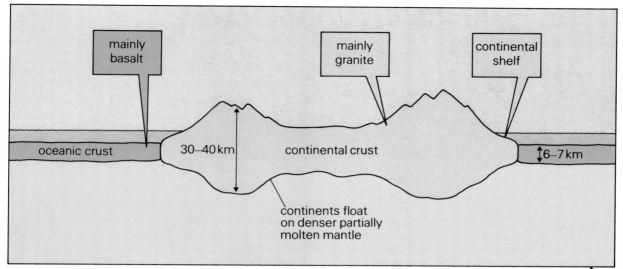

The floating crust

The **crust** is the lightest (least dense) layer of the Earth. *Under the continents* the crust is made up of light rocks such as **granite**. Somewhat denser rocks such as **basalt** occur mainly in the much thinner crust *beneath the oceans*.

Under the light rocks of the crust are the much denser rocks of the **mantle**. *Between* the crust and mantle is a region of *partially molten* mantle. This semi-solid layer is like 'gooey toffee' and it seems to allow the crust to 'float' on the mantle.

The outer and inner core

As shock waves pass through the Earth, they are strongly refracted about 2900 km below the surface. This is the boundary between the mantle and the densest part of the Earth – the **core**.

One kind of shock wave will not travel through a liquid. This wave does not appear to *enter* the core. So the ***outer* core** is probably liquid. Scientists reckon that the outer core contains molten iron and nickel, mixed with a lighter element (silicon or sulphur).

The *other* shock waves that can travel *through* the core speed up and are refracted as they do so. This indicates that there is an even denser layer at the centre of the Earth – this is the solid ***inner* core**, which is thought to be made up of a mixture of solid iron and nickel.

1. How do shock waves help reveal the Earth's structure?

2. Explain why the Earth has not cooled down to a solid lump.

3. The average density of the Earth is 5.5 g/cm^3, while that of the rocks in the crust is 2.7 g/cm^3. What does this tell you about the centre of the planet?

The light continents 'float' on the denser partially molten mantle – like an iceberg on water. ▲

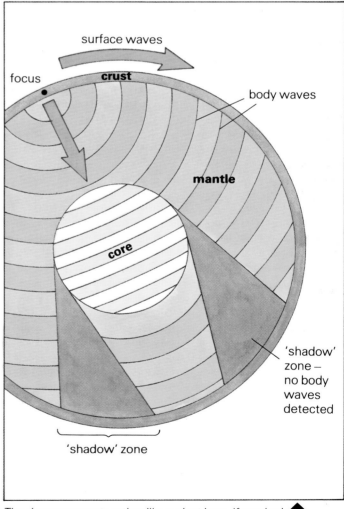

The dense core acts rather like a giant lens, 'focusing' the body waves that pass through it – and creating 'shadow' zones where no body waves can be detected. ▲

5.9   *The record in the rocks*

The Earth's magnetism

The Earth acts like a huge magnet with **magnetic poles** currently a few hundred kilometres away from the *geographic* poles of the Earth's axis. Movements in the liquid metals in the outer core are thought to produce the Earth's magnetic field.

Any magnetic material free to move will lie along the Earth's **magnetic field**. This field acts at an *angle* to the surface, and the angle *varies* from place to place. So magnetic material will lie at an angle to the surface – and this angle indicates the material's position on the surface.

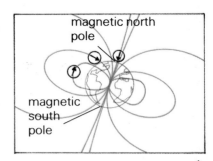

A magnetic record

Magnetic material only stays magnetic up to a temperature known as its **Curie point**. Many rocks contain magnetic materials such as iron. When a rock melts to magma below the crust, its temperature rises above the Curie point for iron and its magnetism is destroyed. If the magma is then pushed back up into the crust, it cools.

Any iron crystals in the solidifying rock become magnetised by the Earth's field. The crystals lie in the direction of the magnetic field *at that place*. So the crystals 'record' where the rock was on the Earth's surface when the rock last solidified.

Earth movements may later shift the rock to a different place – but if the rock doesn't melt again, the rock's magnetic record can reveal its original position.

A magnetic needle points to the magnetic north pole and lies along the Earth's magnetic field. As the compass needle shows, the field is parallel to the Earth's surface at the equator but is straight down at the poles.

The cooling iron crystals set along the Earth's magnetic field. ▼

A magnetic diary

Investigations of the magnetic records in rocks have shown that the Earth's magnetic field is not fixed. The magnetic poles are even *reversed* from time to time – and the magnetic 'north' pole then lies in the geographical south! These changes mean that the magnetic record in a rock also depends on *when* the rock was formed. Rocks with similar magnetic records may have been formed at the same time. Dating one of these rocks by the methods opposite then suggests a date for all of them!

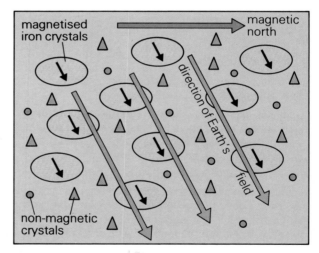

These three blocks of rock, broken by faults, now lie alongside one another – did they always? The rock type and thickness of the layers are the same in each block. But what does the magnetic record tell you about when the blocks were formed? ▼

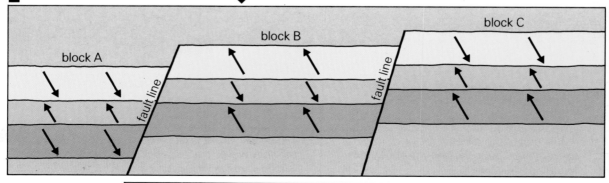

YOU CAN READ MORE ABOUT THE EARTH'S MAGNETISM IN PHYSICS BOOK, SPREAD 5.4.

Radioactive dating

Many rocks contain **radioisotopes** and these provide a more accurate way of dating rocks. As a radioisotope (or 'parent') decays, its atoms change into the atoms of a different isotope (the 'daughter').

The time for *half* the atoms to decay is always the same for a particular radioisotope and is known as its *half-life*. The decay of radioisotopes in a rock can be used to estimate its age.

For example, suppose someone tried to cut down their consumption of chocolates by each day only eating *half* the chocolates still left in a box. The 'half-life of the chocolates' would be one day. If they left the *wrappers* behind (the 'daughters' of the chocolates), the ratio of sweets to wrappers would show you how long the 'diet' had lasted.

In the same way, the *half-life* and ratio of parent to daughter atoms in a rock can be used to date the rock. The remains of living things less than 10 000 years old can be also dated by looking for an active radioisotope called **carbon 14**.

Past life

Sedimentary rocks sometimes contain **fossils** – the remains of plants and animals which lived long ago. To form a fossil, the animal or plant must be buried quickly under sediment – and the sediment must harden to rock. Usually only the *hard* parts of animals and plants are preserved such as bones, shells and bark.

Animals and plants have evolved (changed) over time. Say a certain type of fossil is found in a band of rock which is easily dated. Then in another area, an *identical* fossil is found in another *undated* band of rock. The chances are that the two bands of rock were formed at roughly similar times.

Carbon 14 has a half life of 5700 years, and can be used to date plant and animal remains up to 10 000 years old. This is called **radiocarbon dating**. ▼

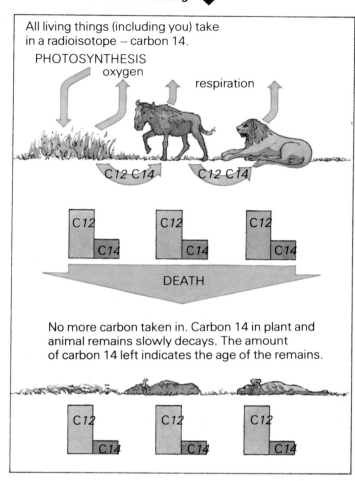

All living things (including you) take in a radioisotope – carbon 14.

No more carbon taken in. Carbon 14 in plant and animal remains slowly decays. The amount of carbon 14 left indicates the age of the remains.

Only a tiny proportion of the countless animals and plants that have lived were preserved as fossils. ▼

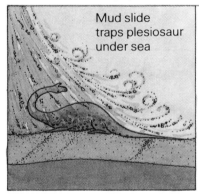

Mud slide traps plesiosaur under sea

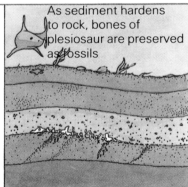

As sediment hardens to rock, bones of plesiosaur are preserved as fossils

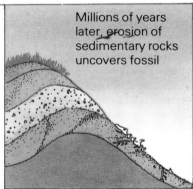

Millions of years later, erosion of sedimentary rocks uncovers fossil

1. At present, a compass needle points roughly north, towards the magnetic north pole. Would this always have been the case in the past? Explain your answer.

2. Why are the strongest magnetic records found mainly in iron-bearing *igneous* rocks?

3. Explain whether you could use the radiosotope carbon 14 to date:
   a. a flint axe-head
   b. the fossil of a dinosaur
   c. an Egyptian wood carving.

YOU CAN READ MORE ABOUT RADIOISOTOPES AND THEIR DECAY ON SPREAD 3.10.

5.10 *The evolving world*

The fossil record

Dating rocks (*see 5.9*) also suggests the ages of any fossils contained – and they, in turn, can be used to date other rocks. This is because life slowly changes or **evolves** over time. A particular fossil only occurs in rocks of a certain age – and any rocks containing it must be that age. For example, rocks containing intricately shaped graptolites must be *older* than rocks containing simpler-shaped graptolites. The millions of fossils discovered allow rocks to be dated easily. They also provide a **fossil record** of life on Earth.

Life evolves in response to changing conditions on the Earth. To survive, animals and plants must adapt to new conditions. Those that fail to do so die out or become **extinct**, while those better suited flourish. The fossil record shows when new creatures evolved and others became extinct. Fossils and other evidence in the rocks have been used to draw up a chart of events in the history of the Earth (*see opposite*). Among the most important events affecting life were the changes in atmosphere and climate.

The evolving atmosphere

The atmosphere of the hot early Earth contained many gases, including steam. As the Earth slowly cooled, water condensed and collected in seas. These absorbed other gases from the air and chemicals from the land to form the 'chemical soup' in which life began. About 3500 million years ago, there was carbon dioxide and other gases in the atmosphere but no free (uncombined) oxygen.

Then the first life – plants – began *taking in* carbon dioxide and *releasing* oxygen during **photosynthesis**. Oxygen reacts easily and so little of this oxygen remained uncombined. It was at least another 2500 million years before there was enough free oxygen for **aerobic respiration** – and animals evolved. Some free oxygen also collected as **ozone**. This absorbs the Sun's ultraviolet rays which would be harmful to life on land. The ozone in the atmosphere allowed life to move on to land. As plants cloaked the bare rock, more and more oxygen was released, and eventually the air became similar to that we breathe today.

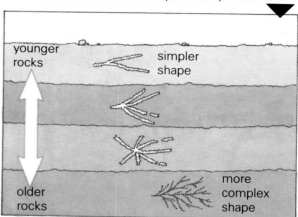

Fossils of the delicate skeletons of graptolites show that these sea animals became simpler in shape over time.

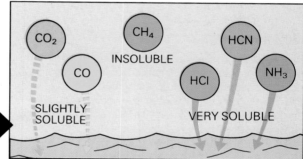

The early atmosphere changed greatly as oceans formed.

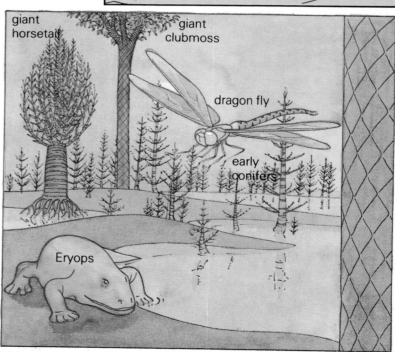

Millions of tonnes of carbon dioxide were 'locked up' in the hot, swampy carboniferous forests – which eventually became the coal we burn today.

Climatic change

The animals and plants that evolved and flourished at a particular time must have been well suited to the climate in that place at that time. So the fossil record gives clues about past climates.

For example, sedimentary rocks formed in the early Cretaceous period contain many shellfish fossils. This suggests there were many shallow warm seas at the time, since shellfish favour these conditions. There have been large variations in climate during **geological time** (the time since the formation of the Earth). These have caused 'population explosions' and extinctions – many such changes are evident in the fossil record.

Geological time

Ideas about events up to 570 million years ago are backed up by scant evidence in the rocks.

By about 570 million years ago, creatures with hard parts had evolved, and these left far more fossils in the rocks. The fossil record for that last 570 million years contains so much information that this time is divided into **eras** and **periods**.

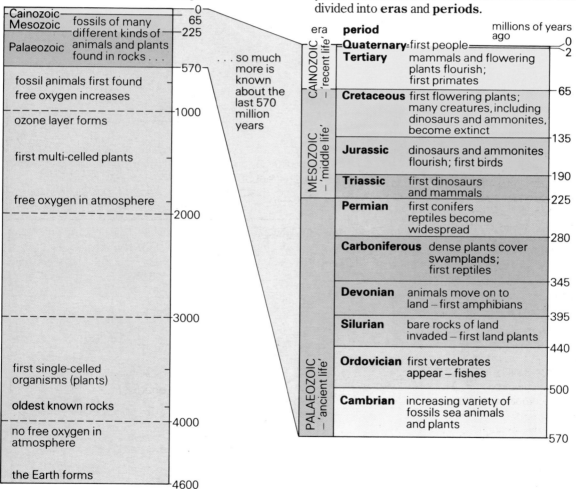

1 Fossils can be used to date rocks. What else can fossils tell us?

2 List some ways in which:
   a changes in the atmosphere affected the evolution of life
   b living things changed the atmosphere.

3 Suggest reasons why:
   a plants had to develop before animals
   b plants had to move on the land before animals could
   c mammals did not flourish until 65 million years ago.

5.11 The Earth's changing face

The continental jigsaw

At the beginning of this century, people believed that the position of the continents never changed. But some were intrigued by the fact that the shapes of South America and Africa fitted together like the pieces of a jigsaw. The German scientist, Wegener, thought this fit was too close to be just chance. He suspected that the continents were *not* fixed – and that South America and Africa had been connected and then drifted apart. He looked for evidence in the rocks that the two continents had once been joined.

Fossil evidence

When land masses are joined, animals and plants can spread freely between them – and the same animals and plants are found on both. When land masses are separated, their animals and plants are *isolated* and evolve *differently*. Yet fossils of the same animals and plants are found on widely separated continents. Wegener claimed these fossils were evidence that the continents were once joined.

Drifting continents?

In 1912, Wegener proposed his **theory of continental drift**. He presented a lot of evidence but could not explain *how* the continents were moved sideways. Most scientists found the idea of drifting continents incredible, and the theory was rejected for decades. But in time new techniques, such as radioactive dating and 'reading' the magnetic record in the rocks, provided further evidence. Investigators found signs that *other* continents have been joined in the past. Eventually, scientists had to accept the theory. It is now thought that continents have come together and drifted apart many times since they formed.

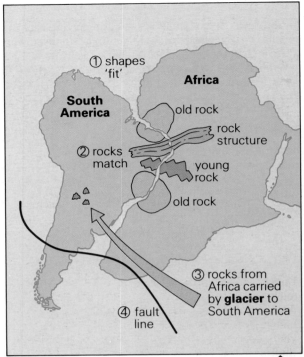

This diagram shows some of the evidence linking Africa and South America. Do you think the two continents were once joined?

Some of the fossil animals and plants found on the two continents. What does this fossil evidence tell you? ▼

	Glossopteris	Mesosaurus	Tyrannosaurus	no fossil horses found in South America	llama
South America					
Africa	Glossopteris	Mesosaurus	Allosaurus	Mesohippus early horse	camel
period of millions of years ago	Carboniferous	Permian	Cretaceous	Tertiary	Quaternary

Evidence

There are several pieces of evidence which indicate that South America and Africa were joined:

- **shapes** 'fit'
- **fossils** of certain ages match
- **rocks** of certain ages match:
  - *chemical analysis* shows rock material matches
  - *dating* (e.g. radioactive) shows rocks same age
  - *magnetic record* shows rocks formed at similar time in similar place
- **faults** continue across both continents
- **climatic records** match:
  - e.g. both have U-shaped valleys formed as *glaciers* moved across continents which were joined

Changing patterns

Fossils and other evidence suggest that some 500 million years ago, Africa, South America, India, Australia and Antarctica formed one huge land mass known as **Gondwanaland**. By about 250 million years ago, *all* the continents were joined together in the 'super continent', **Pangaea**. The drift of the continents about the surface caused changes in the continents' climates. Land that was over the equator could drift towards a pole and become covered in ice. Fossil palm trees have been discovered under London, showing that at one time Britain had a tropical climate.

The spreading ocean

By 1960, the theory of continental drift was accepted but a problem remained – what force could move the vast continents round the face of the Earth? Then some clues were found – under the ocean! North and South America are now separated from Europe and Africa by the Atlantic Ocean. Down the middle of this ocean runs a ridge. Scientists discovered that magma wells up along this ridge and cools to form layers of rock on either side. As more magma wells up, older rock layers are pushed further apart – and the ocean *spreads*. The rate of '**ocean-floor spreading**' can be found by measuring and dating the rock layers. As the Atlantic grows larger, America is moving away from Europe at a rate of about 2 cm a year.

About 200 million years ago, Pangaea began to split up – and the continents slowly drifted to their present positions. ▼

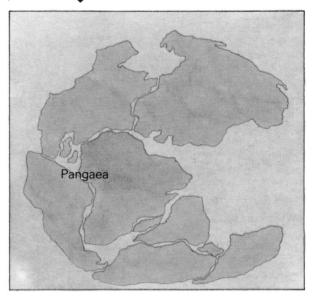

Pangaea

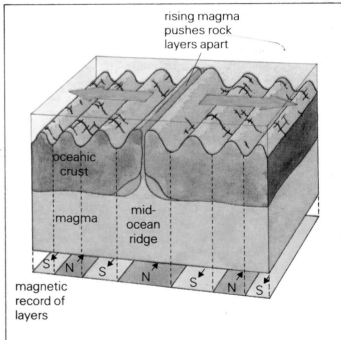

rising magma pushes rock layers apart

oceanic crust

magma

mid-ocean ridge

magnetic record of layers

What evidence is there about the rock layers being pushed apart? ▲

1. Look at the diagram comparing fossils found in Africa and South America. During which ages do you think the continents were:
   a joined?
   b drifting apart?

2. Scientists found Wegener's ideas very difficult to accept. Suggest two reasons for this.

3. Coal and animal fossils have been found under the ice sheets that cover Antarctica. Explain how this is possible.

4. Marsupials (pouched mammals, such as the kangaroo) were once widespread. Now they are mainly found in Australia. Suggest why.

5.12 Plate tectonics

Moving the pieces

Ocean-floor spreading and other discoveries led to the **theory of plate tectonics**. According to this theory, the Earth's crust is cracked up into a small number of gigantic pieces called **plates**. These plates are not fixed; they '*float*' on the partially molten mantle. Heat from the centre of the Earth rises in strong convection currents through the mantle and these currents are thought to cause cracks through weak spots in the crust. The convection currents force hot magma up to the surface. As magma wells up through the crack it pushes apart the crust on either side – and the huge plates are moved sideways.

Colliding plates

Plates are being pushed apart in some parts of the world – so they must be *colliding* in other places. What happens when plates collide depends on the density of their crust. Oceanic crust is much denser than continental crust. When the two collide, the oceanic crust is pushed *beneath* the continental crust, forming a coastal **mountain range** and a deep **trench** in the ocean floor. The rock pushed down melts and becomes less dense, so it floats up towards the crust. This light magma can be forced up through any weaknesses in the crust, creating a volcano or a series of volcanoes.

Convection currents cause cracks in continental crust . . .

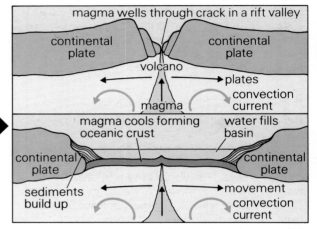

. . . an ocean is born and continents 'drift'.

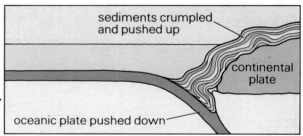

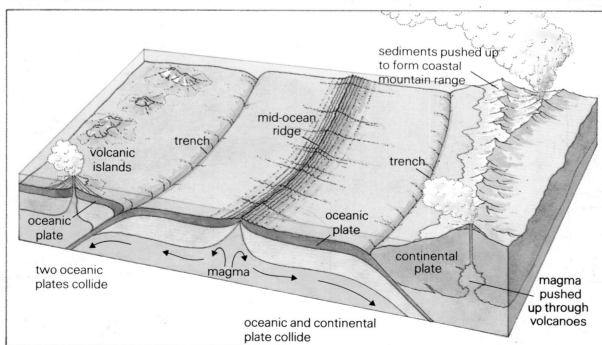

*When oceanic plates collide, one is pushed beneath the other. Sediment scraped off the surface of the descending plate may be forced up, forming an **island arc**. Light magma welling up makes this arc of islands volcanic.*

Folding rock

Only oceanic plates are forced down and 'recycled'. When the thick continental plates move together, neither is pushed below the other. But the collision can cause the sedimentary rock between the plates to buckle up into **fold mountains**. The Alps and the Pyrenees mountain ranges were formed in this way. The Himalayas were created when two great continental plates squeezed the oceanic crust between them up into mountains. ▶

A great theory to fit the evidence!

Before the theory of plate tectonics was proposed, many points about the Earth puzzled scientists. What causes the continents to drift? Why do mountains tend to stretch in long curved chains? Why do volcanoes and earthquakes usually occur only in certain long, narrow areas of the world? The theory was quickly accepted because plate tectonics explains these and many other questions. Mountain building and volcanoes occur at **plate boundaries** between colliding plates. The energy released when plates move gives rise to earthquakes.

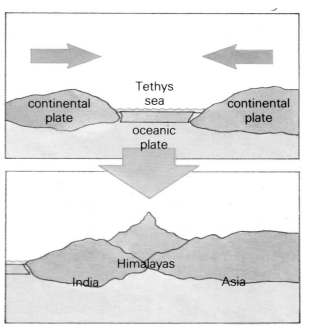

Most volcanic and earthquake activity occurs where the plates collide. ▼

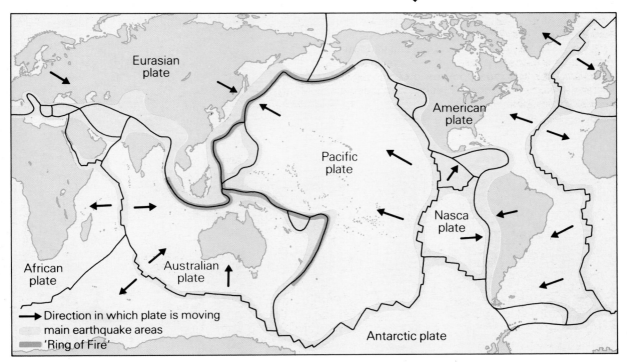

1 Look at the map above, showing the plates.
  a Why do earthquakes occur mainly along plate boundaries?
  b The Rocky Mountains and the Andes run down the west coast of North and South America. Suggest reasons for this. Would you expect them to be fold or volcanic mountains?
  c Why do you think the area marked in red is called 'Ring of Fire'?

  d Would you expect to find a deep oceanic trench near the mid-Atlantic ridge? Explain your answers.

2 What causes the plates and their movement?

3 Why might you find fossil fish on Mount Everest (in the Himalayas)?

Index

Heinemann Educational,
a division of Heinemann Educational Books Ltd,
Halley Court, Jordan Hill, Oxford, OX2 8EJ

OXFORD   LONDON   EDINBURGH
MADRID   ATHENS   BOLOGNA   PARIS
MELBOURNE   SYDNEY   AUCKLAND
SINGAPORE   TOKYO
IBADAN   NAIROBI   HARARE   GABORONE
PORTSMOUTH   NH (USA)

Includes material from *The Sciences for GCSE* first
published 1989–91

This edition first published 1992

ISBN 0 435 57541 4

Designed, illustrated and phototypeset by Gecko
Ltd, Bicester, Oxon

Printed in Spain by Mateu Cromo

The authors and publishers would like to thank the
following for permission to use photographs.

Cover photo: Telegraph Colour Library

Other photos: page 2, top, SPL/Astrid & Hans
Frieder Michler; bottom left, BP; bottom right,
SPL/David Leah; page 3, top, BP and contents
page; middle, ZEFA; bottom, ZEFA/R Marsch;
page 4, top and contents page, ZEFA/Don James;
middle, Ebenezer/Eric Marsh; bottom, ZEFA; page
5 and contents page Ebenezer Pictures/Eric
Marsh; page 6, and contents page, SPL, page 8
Barnaby's Picture Library; page 10, ZEFA; page 16
(×2), Sally & Richard Greenhill; page 17, Trevor
Hill; page 21, J Allan Cash; page 22, top, Frank
Lane Agency/Roger Wilmhurst; middle, Eric and
David Hosking; bottom, GeoScience Features;
page 23, Buildings Research Establishment; page
24, left, John Olive; right, Clare Hayes; page 27
(×3), Clare Hayes; page 28, left, John Olive; right
and bottom, Clare Hayes; page 30, Ann Ronan
Picture Library; page 32 (×5), Clare Hayes; pages
34, 35 and 36 (×10), Clare Hayes; page 38, top
(×6), Clare Hayes; bottom, John Olive; page 40
(×4), Clare Hayes; bottom right, J Allan Cash;
pages 43 and 44 (×5), Clare Hayes; page 48, left,
Barnaby's Picture Library; middle, Sally & Richard
Greenhill; right, Trevor Hill; page 49, David
Redfern/Steve Gillett; page 58, A Michler; page
59, Trevor Hill; page 63, G Muller; page 64, SPL;
page 68, Biophoto Associates; page 73, Trevor
Hill; page 74, left, Environmental Picture Library/C
Westwood; right, Clare Hayes; page 76, SPL;
page 77, Clare Hayes; page 82, Sally & Richard
Greenhill; page 83, Holt Studios; page 84, left,
CEGB; top right, Barnaby's Picture Library; middle
right, Sally & Richard Greenhill; page 85, Colin
Johnson; page 86, left, Barnaby's Picture Library,
left middle, Trevor Hill; right middle, SPL; right
Trevor Hill; page 87, Barnaby's Picture Library;
page 88, top, ZEFA/Abril; middle, bottom and
contents page, GeoScience Features; page 89,
GeoScience Features; page 90, ZEFA; page 91,
Environmental Picture Library/Martin Bond; page
94, Clare Malone; page 96, top, ZEFA; middle,
ZEFA; bottom, Anglesey Aluminium Ltd; page 99,
GeoScience Features; page 102, J Allan Cash;
page 104, H Jalland; page 105, J Allan Cash; page
107, GeoScience Features; page 108 (×2), GSF
Picture Library/Dr B Booth; page 110, GSF Picture
Library.